FLOWERS IN THE DESERT

by

D. M. Larson

For permission to perform the play,
contact doug@freedrama.net

Cast of Characters

JAMIE (female) - A teen-age girl who has run from a conflict at home to stay with her Aunt Betty (MA) in order to have some time to think things out.

SAM (female) - A fun loving teen-age girl who likes to be on top of things. She has a mischievous spirit and loves to joke around. She is madly in love with the neighbor boy (JIMMY).

SARGE (male) - A veteran of the Vietnam War who is in charge of a group home for troubled girls. He is kind hearted but quite firm when things get out of hand.

MA (female) - A strong willed woman who is always in command of every situation. She is loving and keeps things running smoothly, most of the time.

PAULA (female) - A simple teen-age girl who is very enthusiastic about religion and wants to help both people and animals. She tries to be a guiding light and a good example to others but her reasoning ability is sometimes impaired.

SHELLY (female) - A self-declared teen-age beauty queen who appears very in love with herself on the outside, yet feels quite different on the inside.

TINA (female) - An angry teen-age girl who finds reasons to hate everyone. She is good friends with Shelly but doesn't let anyone else get close to her.

JIMMY (male) – Neighbor boy who likes Sam and always gets himself in trouble

CONNIE (female) - Jamie's mother

TOM (male) - Connie's boyfriend

Time and Place
Present day New Mexico. A remote group home for girls.

(A light comes up on a small area of the stage R where SHELLY sits alone doing her hair and looking in a hand mirror)

SHELLY

Beauty and perfection. That's what you are Miss
Shelly. Bet those boys back home would be doing a
quite a bit of howling if they saw you now. Look at all
the wonderful things time has done to you.
(Lowers mirror)
And when I get to Hollywood and become a star,
they'll wonder where this goddess came from. But my
past will be a mystery, because life before this
moment ain't worth telling about. After those early
years things have only gotten better. Actually I'll bet
being born was one of the biggest let-downs of all. I
spent all that time wrapped up in that little space in
my mama, and for what? I pop out and look around,
screaming, wondering if this was such a good idea.
Wondering why someone didn't tell me sooner what it
was gonna be like those first few years, 'cause if
someone had told me, I don't think I woulda come out.

(The light R fades as a light L comes up on PAULA who sits with a baby animal)

PAULA

I've always loved taking care of animals. Horses, cats,
dogs, and especially pigs. Momma Nell, one of my
foster mothers, used to call me that, her little piggy.
And I did look like a little piggy that's for sure. I was
plumper than a Buddha doll. Momma Nell used to
dress me in pink too. I love how she let me call her
Momma.

And pink still is my favorite color. One time Momma
bought me this most beautiful pink dress for a
school. It was all sparkly like pink diamonds. Are
there pink diamonds? And the dress had these big
old puffy shoulders like Cinderella. I felt like a
princess for the whole ride there. I shoulda just
turned and gone home cause that was the best part...

3

PAULA (CONT.)

The boys at the dance said so many mean things to me... they laughed at me... I laughed too... I wanted them to see me laughing... like I wanted to be the joke... I decided piggies shouldn't try to be petunias.
(Smiles, then looks thoughtful and sad)
Momma Nell was the best foster mother I ever had until she got sick. Too sick for me to take care of anymore. I wish they woulda let me try a little longer. I wanted to be there for her like she was for me.
(Puts on a smile)
But I sure know how to take care of animals. That's what I love to do now. I'm like St. Francis of A-sissy.
(Sighs)
And I would sure love to be a saint like Francis, then all this suffering would be worthwhile.

(The light fades and comes up R on TINA)

TINA

I watch TV and see those happy families with the little baby who's takin' its first steps or saying its first word. Them folks make such a big deal out of those things. They laugh, they cry... all 'cause they love their little hairless baboon.
(Pause. Grows sad)
And I sit there all that time and wonder... who was there when I took my first step? Who was there when I said my first word?
(Pause)
I doubt if my first word was mama or papa. I'm sure it was four letters though.
(She chuckles a little, then sighs)
I don't care about them... And they don't care about me. But who really cares anyway.

(The light fades on come up L on SAMANTHA kissing JIMMY. They stop as light comes on and JIMMY takes off. SAM is smiling from ear to ear)

SAMANTHA

I've always liked boys, ever since I could
remember. And they've always liked me. I played post
office and doctor: I loved being the patient. I was
always a big hit at every birthday party, at least until I
got sent home. I never meant any harm. It was always
playing. And nobody has ever minded a little fun.

(The light fades on comes up on MA and SARGE R. SARGE smiles at MA lovingly and MA gives him some gardening stuff and exits)

SARGE

I took this job at the group home so I could help these
girls like nobody helped me. Oh, I had a few people
that helped me along the way, but mostly I was left to
take care of myself. I wasted a lot of years being bitter
and hurting other people who never did nothing to
me. I figure this is my chance to make up for it all.

(Ironic smile)

But helping these girls is like trying to grow flowers in
the desert and that ain't easy.

(Lights fade. Music)

ACT I

Scene 1

(Lights come up on the front of an old farm house. The upstage area is filled with the front of the home which includes a covered front porch and an upstairs window. The door to the home is UC. DR is an area of dirt intended for a garden. The rest of the farm is off stage. PAULA is feeding her baby pig with a bottle)

                    PAULA
Ain't it just the most beautiful mornin'? Ain't it just a
dream? Oh, what a glorious God we have to give us
such a wonderful day.

                    TINA
(Comes out during PAULA's opening speech)

If you start singing, I'm gonna hit you upside the head.

                    PAULA
Well, good morning to you too, Tina. You look nice
today, doesn't she piggy?

                    TINA
You're so weird.

                    PAULA
Off to feed the rest of the animals?

                    TINA
                (Puts on rubber boots)
Unfortunately.

                    PAULA
Oh, that's my favorite job.
                (Baby talk to pig)
I just love feeding the little animals.

                    TINA
                (Pokes pig)
So how's old Oscar Meyer today?

                    PAULA
That's not his name!

6

                    TINA
Well, it should be.
            (PAULA feeds the pig more milk)
That's the way to do it, Paula. Fatten him up. He'll be
ready before you know it.

                    PAULA
Ready for what?

                    TINA
              (Hungry look)
Dinner.

                    PAULA
Hush now. You're gonna scare piggy.

                    TINA
          (Sings as she exits R)
"Oh, I wish I had an Oscar Meyer wiener."

                    PAULA
              (More baby talk)
Don't you pay her no mind, piggy. She's just an awful
little heathen. Yes, she is.

(SARGE enters R with garden tools)

                    SARGE
Morning, Paula.

                    PAULA
Morning, Sarge. What'cha doing?

                    SARGE
I'm going to plant me some flowers right over there.
              (Points DR)

                    PAULA
Well, may God bless your flowers.

(SARGE goes DR, puts on some headphones, turns on his portable music
player, and begins work)

                    TINA
                (Reenters R)
Hey, Sarge. Where's...
                (Sees SARGE)
What's he doing?

                    PAULA
Planting flowers.

                    TINA
In a desert?
                (Yells)
It'll never work, Sarge!

                    PAULA
He can't hear you.
                (Points to ears)
Headphones.

                    TINA
I know that.

                    PAULA
Then why'd you yell?

                    TINA
Cause I felt like it, okay? You got a problem with that?

                    PAULA
No, we don't have a problem, do we piggy?

                    TINA
That's debatable.
                (Looks around)
Where's Ma?

                    PAULA
                (SHELLY comes out of the house)
She went to town to pick up her niece or nephew or
someone like that.

                    SHELLY
                (Smiles)
I hope it's a nephew.

PAULA

How come?

(SHELLY puts on her sunglasses and leans on the porch railing. She lets the morning sun caress her, trying to look like a movie star)

TINA

Why do you ask so many dumb questions?
(PAULA doesn't answer)
When's breakfast going to be? I'm hungry.

PAULA

You slept right through it. We ate before Ma left.

TINA

What?

PAULA

Ma told us to get up early today.

TINA

How come nobody woke me up?

SHELLY

We tried, honey, but you wouldn't budge.

PAULA

Besides, a little fasting always does a person some good.

TINA

Fasting? Are you saying I'm fat or something?

PAULA

No!

TINA

You better not be saying that or I'll bash your face in.

(TINA gives PAULA another dirty look and exits R)

PAULA
(To pig)
I guess she got up on the wrong side of the
trough. She just ain't morning people like us. Isn't that
right, piggy?

SHELLY
(Looking at her clothes)
Paula? Does this color look good on me? I thought it
was pink in the store but now it looks sort of
purple. Oh, but I do like the style of it. It shows off my
finer qualities. I guess the color really doesn't matter
quite so much then does it?
(Very happy)
I can make even a simple little blouse look good, can't
I?

(SHELLY exits back inside)

PAULA
It looked pink to me. Maybe she'll let me borrow it
sometime.
(Baby talk)
Cause pink is our favorite color, ain't it piggy?
(Sad)
Boy, I wish I was as pretty as Shelly.
(Baby talk as she gets up and heads R)
But I guess piggies shouldn't try to be petunias.

(PAULA exits R)

SAM (OFF)
Come and get me, Jimmy boy!

(SAM runs on and is followed by JIMMY)

JIMMY
Why won't you hold still?

SAM
What's the matter? You too slow?

JIMMY
(Points)
Hey, what's Sarge doing?

                    SAM
                  (Looks)
I don't know.

                    JIMMY
                  (Grabs her)
Got ya'.

                    SAM
Not fair!

(Audience can tell SARGE is aware of SAM and JIMMY but SARGE doesn't
let them know)

                    JIMMY
Now for my kiss.

                    SAM
Not in front of Sarge.

                    JIMMY
I don't care about Sarge.

                    SAM
You will when you're dead.
                  (Pushes him away)

                    JIMMY
Just one little kiss?

                    SAM
                  (Pretending to be prissy)
Sorry, I'm not that kind of girl.

                    JIMMY
Yeah, right.

                    MA
                  (Off L)
Here it is, Jamie. Do you need any help with your
bags?

                    JAMIE
                  (Off L)
No, I got them.

                          SAM
It's Ma. You'd better get going.

                         JIMMY
                       (Looks L)
Who's the new girl with Ma? She's kind of cute.

                          SAM
                     (Punches him)
Hey, you watch yourself.

                         JIMMY
What are you going to do about it?

                          SAM
Will you get out of here?

                         JIMMY
You gonna make me?

(SAM grabs JIMMY's ear and drags him off R. SARGE snickers quietly to
himself)

                     JIMMY (CONT.)
Ow. Ow.

                          MA
                  (Enters L with JAMIE)
We're still in the process of fixing it up.

                         JAMIE
                     (Being polite)
It's nice.

                          MA
Not really. But once we put some time into it, we'll get
it looking pretty good.

                         JAMIE
I see.

                          MA
Here. Let me take your bags inside for you.
                     (Takes her bag)

JAMIE

Thank you.

MA

I'll put your bag in my room for now. Did you bring anything valuable?

JAMIE

Huh?

MA

I like to believe the best about our girls here at the group home, but sometimes nice things tempt them and those nice things disappear.

JAMIE
(Nervous)
No, I don't think I have anything like that.

MA

Sorry, Jamie. I don't mean to scare you. They're really nice girls once you get to know them. Some of them have pretty rough edges but after time you'll see how neat they can be.

SHELLY
Ma!
(Holds up a scarf)
Look what Paula did to my new scarf! It looks like she dropped it in cow manure!

MA

Now, Shelly. Calm down.
          (Takes scarf with two cautious finger)
It should wash out.

SHELLY
I could kill her. I could just kill her.
          (Exits inside)

MA

I better take care of this before it turns into another Pearl Harbor.
          (Points DR)
Go say hi to your Uncle Joe and ask him to introduce you to some of the girls.

JAMIE
(Very nervous)
How many girls are there in your group home?

MA
(Smiles)
Only four.
(As she exits into house)
Relax, Jamie. Everything will be fine.

(JAMIE goes to SARGE and taps him on the shoulder)

JAMIE

Uncle Joe?

SARGE
(Takes off headphone)
Well, hey there, Jammer? I heard you were
coming. How's my favorite niece?

JAMIE

Okay, I guess.

SARGE
Just okay, huh? Something eating you?

JAMIE

Not really.
(Looking around nervously)

SARGE
(Looks around too. Whispers)
What you looking for?

JAMIE

Huh? Oh, nothing.

SARGE
Nervous about meeting the girls?

JAMIE
(Gives a "how did you read my mind" look)
Uh... no.

SARGE
(Responding to her actions rather than words)
Don't worry. They're nice girls if you give them half a
chance.
(Looks around)
Have you met any of them yet?

JAMIE
No, but it's okay. I can meet them later. There's no
hurry.

SARGE
I should get at least one of them to show you around.

JAMIE
I'm kind of a loner. I can find my way around.

SARGE
(Takes a good look at her)
Is something wrong? You seem a lot different from
the last time I saw you.

JAMIE
It's been awhile.

SARGE
Not that long. Is something wrong?

JAMIE
I don't really want to talk about it, okay Uncle Joe?

SARGE
(Knowing when to back off)
Okay.
(Looks off R)
Oh, good. Here comes Sam.

JAMIE
I better go inside and unpack.

SARGE
(Gently grabs JAMIE)
Sam, come over here. I want to introduce you.

SAM
(Enters R)
I kinda got something else to do, Sarge.

SARGE

Like what?

SAM

Never mind.

SARGE

Jamie. Meet Samantha.

SAM

Don't call me that name. You know I hate that.

SARGE

Sorry Sandpaper.

SAM
I don't think I like my nickname much better.
          (Goes to JAMIE. Looks at SARGE)
My friends call me Sam.
                    (Looks over JAMIE)
What are you in for?

SARGE
Sam! You know better than to talk like that.

SAM

Sorry.

SARGE
She's our niece. She's here for a visit.

SAM

Why?

SARGE
Some people actually like to come see us.

                              SAM
                      (Sly look at SARGE)
I don't see why.
                  (SARGE rolls his eyes but smiles)
Does she talk?

                             JAMIE
Yes.

                              SAM
Well, she knows one word.

                             JAMIE
                        (Getting upset)
Can I go inside now, Sarge?

                             SARGE
                  (Gives SAM an annoyed look)
Sure, Jamie.
                   (JAMIE goes quickly inside)
What was that all about?

                              SAM
What do you mean?

                             SARGE
Why did you go and pick on her like that?

                              SAM
                        (Looks away)
I wasn't...

                             SARGE
Yes, you were. And you're going to make up for it.

                              SAM
How?

                             SARGE
You're going to become Jamie's best pal while she's
here.

                              SAM
But Sarge...

SARGE

She can even stay in your room.

SAM

What? Roommates with Shelly AND the geekazoid?

SARGE

No. I will give in on that point. Shelly will move in with
Tina. And if you're nice to Jamie the whole time she's
here then Shelly stays with Tina when Jamie leaves.

SAM

What if Jamie never goes?

SARGE

She won't be staying that long.

SAM

Oh, that's right. She has a family to go home to.

SARGE

Just a mother.

SAM

That's more than I have.

SARGE

Will you do it?

SAM
(Pause. Thinks about it)
Sure. Why not? Anything to get rid of Shelly.

SARGE
(Tries to give SAM a hug)
You're a good kid, Sandpaper.

SAM
(Squirms)
I know.

SARGE

After morning devotions, show her around.

SAM

Does that mean no chores?

SARGE

Don't push it, Sam.

SAM

Don't worry, I will.

MA
(Comes out with SHELLY. MA
carries a small devotion book)
Devotion time.

SAM

Ah, do we have to do devotions every morning? Even God took a rest once in a while.

MA

Do you have to complain about it every morning? You know we always do them.
(To SHELLY)
Would you go get Paula and Tina?

SHELLY

Out in the barn? But I'm not dressed for it.

SARGE

And why aren't you? You have barn duty today.

SHELLY

I do? Are you sure?

SARGE

I'm sure.

SAM

She knows she has barn duty. She just wanted to show off her new clothes.

SHELLY

I did not.

SAM

Did so.

                    MA
Girls. Stop. Shelly, you go change so you can do your
chores right after devotions. Sam. Would you go get
the others?

                    SAM
            (Snotty look at SHELLY)
I would love to.

(SAM exits R)

                    MA
And Shelly? Could you ask Jamie to come out too?
            (SHELLY nods and exits
                through UC door)
Sometimes, those girls...

                    SARGE
Probably having someone new around is setting them
off.

                    MA
And Jamie was acting really upset when she came
in. What happened out here?

                    SARGE
Sam was giving her a hard time. I took care of it.

                    MA
I hope so because something is really bothering
Jamie and I want her to feel like this is a safe enough
place to talk about it.

                    SARGE
Her visit sure came out of the blue. Did your sister
have something come up?

                    MA
I haven't talked to my sister yet about it. I only talked
to Jamie on the phone last night. I didn't get to talk to
her mother.

                    SARGE
Strange.

                        MA
You think so?

                       SARGE
Just a little.

                        MA
I thought it was too, but I figure it was just me.

                       SARGE
Has she told you anything out of the ordinary yet?

                        MA
No, she simply said she wanted to visit and I've left it
at that.

                       SARGE
I guess that could be all there is to it.
                      (Joking)
This is such a wonderful vacation spot.

                        MA
It is if you like rattlesnakes.

                        SAM
They're coming.

                       TINA
                   (Off. Sings)
"I wish I had an Oscar Meyer wiener."

                       PAULA
               (Enters. Carrying Pig)
I don't hear you.

                       TINA
                   (Comes on)
Here, piggy, piggy. Time for dinner.

                       PAULA
It is not.

                        MA
Paula, will you please leave that pig in the barn? It's
not a baby.

PAULA

Yes, it is. It's my baby.

TINA

You know, she's right. They even look alike.

PAULA

Can't piggy at least stay for devotions?

SAM

What for? Animals don't have souls.

PAULA

They do too.

SAM

Do not.

PAULA

How would you know?

SAM

I live with enough of them.

TINA

Are you calling me an animal?

SAM

If the feed bag fits...

MA
(Looks through book)
Maybe we need an extra-long devotion today.

SAM
(SAM straightens up)
No, that's okay. Sorry, Tina.

TINA

You better be.

PAULA
(Pouting)
I'll go put piggy back.

(PAULA exits R)

                         MA
Sam. Would you get Shelly now?

                         SAM
                       (Yells)
HEY, SHELLY! GET OUT HERE NOW!

                         MA
That's not quite what I had in mind.

(SHELLY and JAMIE come out)

                         SAM
                   See it worked.

                        SHELLY
We were almost out here anyway. Sorry I took so
long.
                   (Smiles at JAMIE)
Jamie and I were just getting to know each other.

                         MA
Everyone come sit down. Sarge? Would you read this
morning?

                        SARGE
                    (Takes book)
         Sure.

                        SHELLY
                 (Whispers to JAMIE)
This should take forever.

                         MA
                     (Hears her)
         Do you want to read?

(SHELLY looks away)

                     MA (CONT.)
         Go ahead, Sarge.

                        SARGE
         "In death, we find life."

                        SAM
Cheery title.

                        MA
Sh.

                       SARGE
                (Reads with difficulty)
"In everyday living, we... encounter... difficult...
situations. We... struggle with the ups and downs of
day to day living and sometimes we get so...
overwhelmed we want it all to end. Nothing seems to
go right for us and we feel like it never will. Some
people see death as the answer. And in one kind of
death you can find a way out."

                       SHELLY
What's that again?

                        MA
Oh, good. You girls do listen.

                       SARGE
"Suicide is of course the wrong way out. The kind of
death we should seek is the end to our old ways of
living. We should let our old ways die and seek..."

                       SHELLY
                      (Mocking)
"Eternal life in Jesus Christ." These things always end
the same way.

MA
There's a reason for that, Shelly.

                       SHELLY
But it seems so... fake.

                        SAM
You're one to talk.

                       SHELLY
What's that supposed to mean?

                        SAM
Nothing.

PAULA

Be quiet you two. You're ruining a good devotion.

SHELLY

There's no such thing as a good devotion.

SARGE

Now, Shelly...

SHELLY

Oh, shut up, Sarge. Just shut up.

(SHELLY runs off R)

SARGE
(Angry)

You come back here!

(SARGE starts after her. MA stops him)

MA

Let me go. You calm down.

(SARGE nods. MA exits R. SARGE throws down book and exits L)

PAULA

Sarge.
                    (Picks up book and dusts it off)
You didn't finish.

SAM

I don't think he wants to.

PAULA

Of course he does. I better go talk to him.

TINA

I wouldn't if I were you. He's so mad, he'll probably
smack you.

PAULA

He would not.

TINA

Don't say I didn't warn you.

(TINA exits inside)

PAULA
Maybe I'll wait.

(PAULA goes inside too)

JAMIE
Are things always like this around here?

SAM
(Deciding to be nice)
Yes, most of the time.

JAMIE
It must be hard.

SAM
It's better than nothing. At least we have a place to
live.

JAMIE
What do you mean? People always have some place
to live.

SAM
Are you sure we're living on the same planet? Haven't
you heard of the homeless?

JAMIE
Yes, but they're just junkies and stuff. You never see
kids homeless.

SAM
You don't get out much do you?

JAMIE
What do you mean?

SAM
Nothing.

JAMIE
No, come on. Tell me.

SAM

Okay, I'll tell you. Homeless kids aren't homeless because they want to be. Homeless kids are usually ones that aren't wanted. Either their parents died or they left them. Oh, sure there's foster homes but they don't really want you either. If they did, why would they keep getting rid of me?

I didn't always have a home. I lived on the streets a little while. And surprise, there were lots of kids there with me. People never thought we were homeless even though we weren't dressed nice. Kids never dress nice anyway. And sometimes we'd even get a five finger discount on something nice from a store. That's how I got caught. I hadn't been out there very long when they got me. Some kids are out there forever. They learn how to survive. I didn't.

They gave me a choice. Come here to the Happy Rancher or go to jail. Sarge even came down to visit with me.

(Softens)

He told me about the Happy Rancher and despite the stupid name it sounded kinda cool. And he did something most people never did for me. He asked me what I wanted. He really wanted to know what he could help me do for myself. I just broke down and cried. It seemed like I cried forever. I'd finally found someone who cared.

(Realizes she's just spilled
her guts to a stranger and
makes a total turn around)

Oh, man, what am I saying. You must think I'm a total dork.
(Laughs)

Real sob story, huh? It wasn't that big of deal.

JAMIE

Sam, you don't have to put on an act for me. I'm glad you shared that with me.

                    SAM
Don't get all mussy on me okay.
                         (Looks around)
So. Do you want the grand tour?

(JAMIE is confused about SAM's changes in attitude)

                    JAMIE
Okay.

                    SAM
                  (Points DL)
Over there is the road in. It's so long you can't hardly
see the main road.
                    (Point L)
Over there is the garage.
                  (Smiles slyly)
And Jimmy's house.

                    JAMIE
Who's Jimmy?

                    SAM
He's just a real good friend of mine.

                    JAMIE
Oh.

                    SAM
                  (Points DR)
That's Sarge's garden.
                  (Points R)
Over there is the barn where Shelly's balling her eyes
out.
                  (Points UC)
And this here is our lovely home.

                    JAMIE
Thanks for the tour.

                    SAM
No problem.

                    JAMIE
I wonder if Shelly's okay.

SAM

She's never okay.

JAMIE

What do you mean? She seemed pretty nice on the
whole.

SAM
(Surprised)
Oh, don't tell me you fell for you little act.
(Imitates SHELLY)
"Don't you just love my hair? Ain't I just the most
beautiful thing you've laid eyes on?"
(Back to self)
Don't you think she's just a little too stuck on herself?

JAMIE

Maybe just a little.

SAM

Don't worry. Old Tami Fay's true colors will show
more and more as time goes on. She can only put
that act on for so long. And you should try seeing
Shelly without all that makeup. Now that's scary.

JAMIE

I sure didn't like the way she acted a few minutes ago
though.

SAM

I know. One minute she's Miss Perfect and the next
minute she's Psycho. I'm always calling her Jeckle
and Heidi.

JAMIE

Here they come.

MA
(Enters R with SHELLY)
Wait here. I'll get Sarge.

SAM

Sarge went towards the garage.

MA

Thanks.

SAM

So Shelly, you ready to get it?

SHELLY
(Cool and calm)

I don't know what you mean.

SAM

Sarge is sure mad at you. You shouldn't push
Vietnam vets around like that you know.
(Creeps up to SHELLY)
Cause one day, you're going to push him too far.
(Tries to scare SHELLY)
And he's gonna snap!

SHELLY
(The ice queen)

Don't be silly.

MA
(Enters with SARGE)

Okay, Shelly.

SHELLY
(Unemotional)

I'm sorry that I told you to shut up.

SARGE
(Doesn't look at SHELLY. Speaks to MA)

You'll take care of her punishment.

MA
I will.
(To SHELLY)

See me after your chores.
(SHELLY gives a slight nod)

SARGE
(To MA)

Send the other girls out here. It's time for chores.
(MA exits into house)
Shelly, you have barn duty.

SHELLY

I knew I should have waited to do my hair. And it
looks so nice today.

SARGE

You'll also want to move all your things out of Sam's
room. Jamie's going to stay with her.

SHELLY

And where am I moving to?

SAM
(Mock sincerity)
I'm afraid you're going to have to stay in the barn,
Shelly.

SHELLY
(Loses her cool)

What?!

SARGE

Samantha.

SAM

Sorry.

SARGE

You're moving in with Tina.

SHELLY
(Excited)

Yes.

SARGE

But after what you pulled today, I'm not sure the barn
is such a bad idea.

SHELLY

I said I was sorry.

SARGE

Sometimes sorry isn't enough.

SHELLY

It never is with you.

(SHELLY exits R. SARGE restrains himself)

                    TINA
                (From inside)
Oink! Oink!

                    PAULA
                (Runs out)
Stop!

                    TINA
                (Comes out)
Oink, oink, oink.

                    PAULA
Make her stop, Sarge.

                    SARGE
Tina, go finish feeding the animals and help Shelly
with the barn when you're done.

                    TINA
Oink.
                (Exits R)
Oink, oink, oink.

                    SAM
I see Tina's getting back to her roots.

                    PAULA
What can I do for you today, Sarge?

                    SARGE
You're on garden duty.

                    PAULA
                (In heaven)
Cultivating God's garden. I shall keep it as clean as
Eden.

                    SAM
Before or after they ate the apple?

                    PAULA
I didn't hear that.

(PAULA exits R)

                        SARGE
                        (To SAM)
You're inside today.

                        SAM
Okay. I'll catch you later, Jamie.

                        JAMIE
Bye. Thanks for the tour.

                        SAM
No problem.

(SAM exits inside)

                        SARGE
Are you and Sam getting along?

                        JAMIE
I guess so.

                        SARGE
It'll take time to get through all the rough stuff but
she's a pretty neat kid underneath it all.

                        JAMIE
She seems to really like you too.

(MA comes out)

                        SARGE
Yeah, we do seem to get along. I wish I could say the
                        same about Shelly.

                        MA
Jamie? Could you run inside and help Sam a minute?

                        JAMIE
Uh, okay.

                        MA
Thanks.

(JAMIE goes inside)

MA (CONT.)

So how are you doing?

SARGE

Not so good. Why can't I get through to Shelly?

MA

For the same reason I can't always get through to
Sam. Some people simply get along better than
others. You and Sam have a special connection I'll
never have with her.

SARGE

That's fine if you get along better with Shelly than I do,
but Shelly seems to outright hate me.

MA

Sam may not hate me, but she sure tries to find ways
to get under my skin. Just now she ran in the house
and told me you were so fed up with Shelly that you
were out here trying to drown her in the trough. She
got me so worked up I ran to the window to look.

(SARGE is trying not to laugh)

MA (CONT.)

Yes, she thought it was pretty funny too. Well I didn't.

SARGE

Okay, you've made your point.

MA

Do you feel better then?

SARGE

A little. I still wish I could find out what she doesn't like
about me. I mean she doesn't have to like me or
anything. I just want to know what I did.

MA

You may not have done anything. Give it time.
(SARGE nods)
I better get back inside and watch Sam. I wonder
what she has up her sleeve next.

(SARGE laughs and MA exits. He puts his headphones on and goes to his flowers. SAM comes out to shake off a rug)

                    JIMMY
(Appears cautiously from UL corner of house)
Pst. Hey, Sam.

                    SAM
Jimmy. What are you doing here?

                    JIMMY
I missed you.

                    SAM
                (Shakes off rug)
I saw you less than an hour ago.

                    JIMMY
I came back for my kiss.

                    SAM
Tough. I'm busy.

                    JIMMY
But I need you, Sam.

                    SAM
I think you'll survive.

                    JIMMY
Come on, Sam. You can't make a guy wait like
this. It's all biological you know.

                    SAM
I never heard our biology teacher say anything about
it.

                    JIMMY
Old frog eyed Ferguson doesn't know nothing about
these things. I'm surprised he even knew enough to
have kids.

                    SAM
Maybe he did it asexually.

                          JIMMY
A-what?

                          SAM
Don't you ever listen in school?

                          JIMMY
I musta been gone that day.

                          SAM
You're gone every day.

                          JIMMY
                    (Goes to her)
Just one teenie-tiny kiss?

                          SAM
                  (Shakes rug at him)
No.

                          MA
          (Comes out. Followed by JAMIE)
What is taking you so long?
                    (Sees JIMMY)
Oh, hello, Jimmy. What are doing around here today?

                          JIMMY
I... uh... was wondering if you had any work for me
today?

                          SAM
Nice save.
          (JIMMY gives SAM a dirty look as she exits)

                          MA
You'll have to ask Sarge.
(Points at SARGE at flowerbed)

                          JIMMY
Thanks.
          (MA exits. He looks over JAMIE)
Well, hello there. Who might you be? No wait. Let me
guess your name. I'm pretty good at it. Let's see...
Cindy? Candy? Mandy?

JAMIE
(Unimpressed)
It's Jamie.

JIMMY
Pretty name.
(He smiles at her)
And you're pretty too.

JAMIE
So how long have you and Sam been together?

JIMMY
Oh, come on. Let me have my fun.

JAMIE
You're not my type.

JIMMY
You're a frisky one, ain't you?

JAMIE
Frisky? Excuse me. I think I need to be someplace
else.

JIMMY
I'll catch you later.

(JIMMY winks. JAMIE rolls her eyes and exits into house. JIMMY goes over
to SARGE)

JIMMY (CONT.)
Howdy, Sarge!

(JIMMY's yelling makes SARGE jump)

SARGE
I don't have them on that loud, Jimmy.

JIMMY
Sorry.

SARGE
What you need?

                        JIMMY
Got any work for me today?

                        SARGE
Not that I can think of. Drop by later though. I might
have you go into town with me to pick up some feed.

                        JIMMY
Sounds good.

(SARGE starts back to work. Pause. JIMMY thinks then speaks)

                    JIMMY (CONT.)
Maybe Sam could come along. We could use the
help.

                        SARGE
                (Stops. Looks at JIMMY)
I don't know. She might be busy helping Ma.

                        JIMMY
That's okay. No biggie.
                (Embarrasses, disappointed)

                        SARGE
We'll see. Sam always likes to go to town. Maybe she
can run some errands for Ma.

                        JIMMY
                        (Happy)
Okay. Just let me know.

                        SARGE
See you, Jimmy.

(JIMMY runs off L. SARGE smiles and puts back on headphones. SAM and
JAMIE come out with a big rug to shake out)

                        SAM
Shoot. I missed him.

                        JAMIE
Jimmy's sure is different.

                           SAM
He's the only male within a million miles of here, so I
make do.

                           JAMIE
I suppose I'd get desperate too.

                           SAM
He's not that bad. He seems like a real jerk
sometimes, but deep down there's something good. I
think that's true of most people.

(Pause. Thinks)

Except maybe Shelly... and Tina... and Fred from
church ain't so good... oh, well I guess maybe it's
about 50-50.

                           JAMIE
I seems that way.

                           SAM
Actually Jimmy and I are getting pretty serious.

(SARGE perks up, but tries to not to listen)

                           JAMIE
You are?

                           SAM
Get a load of this?

                    (Holds out hand)

It's a promise ring. We're darn near engaged.

                           JAMIE
What do Ma and Sarge think about that?

                           SAM
It's none of their business.
                    (Looks at ring)
Do you think these are diamonds?

(Shows JAMIE the ring. JAMIE looks really close)

                    JAMIE
Where?

                    SAM
Next to the emerald.

                    JAMIE
              (Trying to be nice)
Uh, I can't tell.

                    SAM
He says they are.
              (Looks at her ring proudly)
I bet he spent a fortune on this.

(SARGE quietly chuckles)

                    JAMIE
I'll bet he did.

                    SAM
Now that I've shared all my deep dark secrets, how
about telling me some of yours.

                    JAMIE
I don't really have any to tell.

                    SAM
Everyone has a story.

                    JAMIE
I'm afraid there's nothing to tell.

                    SAM
What about why you're here?

                    JAMIE
What do you mean?

                    SAM
You're not really here for just a visit, are you?

                    JAMIE
How did you...

(SARGE is really listening now)

SAM

I've been around Jamie. I'm not stupid.

JAMIE

I guess not.

SAM

So come on. Spill it.

JAMIE

I don't really want to talk about it.

SAM

Oh, it must be good. Let me guess. You're pregnant?

JAMIE

No!

SAM

You were caught shoplifting?

JAMIE
(Annoyed)
No, Sam. Nothing like that.

SAM

You had a bad hair day and your friends made fun of you.

JAMIE

Now you're making fun of me.

SAM

I'm sorry. I won't say another word about it. I won't even ask a question again. About anything. Anything at all.

JAMIE

Fine. Do you want to hear my big secret?

SAM
(Desperate)
Please.

JAMIE

Yesterday, I packed up my bags, hopped on a bus, and left home for good.

SAM

You ran away, huh?

JAMIE

You sound disappointed.

SAM

I was hoping for something a little more exciting.

JAMIE

I couldn't stand living there anymore. Not as long as mom stays with that jerk.

SAM

Wicked stepfather, huh?

JAMIE

Sort of. They're not married... yet.

MA
(Comes out)
How long does it take to shake out a rug anyway? This is going to take us all day.

JAMIE

Sorry, we got to talking.

SAM

We've been sharing our darkest secrets.

MA

Oh, dear. That doesn't sound good.

SAM
(Gets a weird look on her face)
No. It wasn't.
(JAMIE and SAM go inside)

MA
(Shakes out a small rug)
At least they're getting along.

SARGE
(Takes off headphones)
You think those kids would learn by now.

MA
(Goes to him)
What are you talking about?

SARGE
I heard their secrets.

MA
(Interested)
You did?
(Realizes she's an adult)
You shouldn't listen to them like that, Joe.

SARGE
I guess you don't want to know what they said then.

MA
I didn't say that.

SARGE
I didn't overhear anything new with Sam but Jamie did
say why she's here.

MA
She ran away because she doesn't like the man her
mother is seeing.

SARGE
How do you know that?

MA
I just called Jamie's mother. Jamie left a note for her
mom telling her why she left but her mom didn't know
where Jamie went.

SARGE
So much for my career as a spy.

MA
Connie was sure glad to hear that Jamie's with us.

SARGE

I'll bet. So is Connie coming to get her?

MA

She wanted to but I told her to give it some time. I think Jamie might come around on her own.

TINA
(Enters R)
Hey, Sarge. Can I take a break and go get the mail?

SARGE

As long as you're more than half-way done. I do have other things for you to do.

TINA

I'll be done. Can I drive the truck down?

SARGE

I guess...
(Tosses her the keys)
Keep it under 30.

TINA

You're no fun.

(Exits L)

SARGE

One of these days, one of the girls is going to run off on me.

MA

They have. Don't you remember our first year here?

SARGE

I've been trying to forget.

MA

I swear we spent half our time chasing those girls down.

SARGE

But when your only choice is jail or here, I know where I'd be. I wish they would have had some place like this for me when I was a kid. It may've kept me out of trouble.

MA
(Smiles and laughs)
Probably not.

SARGE
(Looks at watch)
It is about time for break, isn't it?

MA
Maybe not for Sam though. Every time I turn around she's taking a break.

SARGE
Besides the girls will want to get their mail. Some of them really look forward to it.

MA
Some of them look forward to it too much.

SARGE
I'll go get Paula and Shelly. Maybe I'll even surprise Shelly and finish up for her out there.
(Exits R)

MA
And I suppose I'll get Sam.
(Exits inside)

PAULA
(Off)
Thank you, Sarge. I'm expecting some important information.
(Enters R)
I sure hope it comes today.

SAM
(Comes from house with JAMIE)
A break already? Seems like we've hardly worked at all.

JAMIE
I think we've spent most of the time talking.

SAM
(Trying to look serious and tough)
I've been working and nobody is going to know different are they? It's our little secret.

JAMIE
(Laugh)
Uh-huh, okay.

SAM
(Like a gangster)
You're a good kid. I like you. I think I'll keep you around.

SHELLY
(Enter R dirty and annoyed)
Look at me. What a mess.
(Almost in tears)
And I broke a nail too.

PAULA
(Goes to her)
Let me see. Poor, Shelly.

SHELLY
(Moves away)
I don't need your sympathy, Paula.

SAM
What Shelly needs is a demolition crew.

SHELLY
Do I look that bad?

SAM
Let's just say that Frankenstein had better hair days.

SHELLY
Oh, and I had my hair perfect today.

PAULA
Don't listen to Sam. You never look bad.

SHELLY
And what do you know, Paula. You can't even wear clothes that are color coordinated.

SAM

Man, Shelly. What did Paula ever do to you?

PAULA

Its okay, Sam. She's upset. She doesn't mean it.

TINA
(Enters L)

Speedy delivery.

PAULA

Here, let me see.

SHELLY

Did I get a letter?

TINA

Back off, girls. I'll call off the names. And if you want
the letter, that will be a dollar.

PAULA

But I don't have...

SAM

She's joking, Paula.

TINA

Sure I am. If you don't have a dollar, you can wrestle
me for it.

SHELLY

Hurry up, Tina.

TINA

Okay.
                (Goes through mail)
A big envelope for Paula.
        (PAULA reaches for it and TINA pulls away)
It's from Oral Roberts University.

SAM

Isn't he the one that asked for all that money and said
God would kill him if he didn't get it?

TINA
(Still keeping it from PAULA)
The very same.

JAMIE
You're kidding. Did he get the money?

SAM
I don't know, did he?

PAULA
Yes, he did. Now give it here.

SAM
I can't believe people for stuff like that. What kind of
idiot would give him money?

PAULA
I did. I didn't want him to die.

TINA
That is truly pathetic.

PAULA
Give me my mail.

TINA
I wanna look at it. What kind of classes do they offer
there anyway? Con-artist 101? Money making ideas
201? Maybe I should go there to.

PAULA
They probably wouldn't let you in. They don't take
mean people.

TINA
(Pretend shock)
I've been insulted. Paula actually insulted me.

SAM
Will you give Paula her stupid mail please?

SHELLY
Yeah, I want to see what I got.

(TINA gives envelope to PAULA who sits on porch and excitedly reads it)

TINA

Let's see.
(Looks through mail)
Sarge, Ma, Sarge, Jamie.
(Holds out letter)

SAM

Jamie?

TINA
(JAMIE comes to take it)
One dollar, please.
(Smiles)
Just joking.

(Hands it over)

SAM

Who's it from?

JAMIE

My mother. How'd she know I was here?

SAM

Lucky guess?

JAMIE

Or Aunt Betty told her?

TINA

A letter for Shelly. Which boy is it this time?

SHELLY
(Grabs it)
The only boy there is.

SAM

Ew. Not Fred.

SHELLY

Freddie happens to be a very loving person.

SAM

I know that he sure loves to pick his nose. He's always up in the front row mining for gold. I wonder if he grosses out the pastor.

(TINA tries not to let SHELLY see her laugh)

                    SHELLY
At least my boyfriend is clean.

                    SAM
What is that supposed to mean?

                    SHELLY
I can smell Jimmy coming before I ever see him.

                    SAM
Oh, shut up Miss Primps-a-lot.

                    TINA
All right. Here's my Sci-Fi Magazine. Check this out.

(SAM and JAMIE come to look)

                    JAMIE
How'd they get him to look like that?

                    TINA
Read and find out.

                    SAM
I think I'll pass.
                    (Takes rest of mail)
How come I never get anything?
                    (Stops at a letter)
Hey, what's this?

                    JAMIE
Somebody returned a letter to Uncle Joe.

                    SAM
It's to Vietnam. And it's to a woman.

                    TINA
Let me see.
                    (Takes envelope)
How can you tell it's a woman? All those Asian names
are alike.

                         PAULA
You leave that letter alone.

                         SAM
                    (Takes it back)
I wonder who it is.

                         PAULA
I'm gonna tell.

                         TINA
You tell and I'll bash in your face.

                         SAM
Don't worry. We won't look at it.

                         TINA
We won't?

                         SAM
See, Paula. There it goes back in the pile. All safe
and sound.

                         PAULA
Good.

(PAULA exits inside. SAM winks at TINA and take letter out again. She puts
it inside her shirt)

                         SHELLY
That rat!

                         TINA
What is it, Shelly?

                         SHELLY
That dirty, stinking sorry excuse for a...

                         TINA
What did he say?

                         SHELLY
                    (In tears)
Look at the letter he wrote me.

TINA

"Dear Shelly, I got your letter and picture. My friends
and I got a great laugh out of the letter. Thanks."

SHELLY

I want to kill him.

TINA

"Did you really think I liked you? You're cute and all
but I don't think you could be my girlfriend. I'm sure
you know why."

JAMIE

What does he mean by that?

SAM

He means that he doesn't want a girlfriend who lives
in a group home.

JAMIE

Why not?

SAM

Cause we're not good enough, Jamie.

SHELLY

I want him dead.

JAMIE

But that's not true. There's nothing wrong with you.

SAM

Tell that to them. They seem to think so.

SHELLY

I want to cut him up into little pieces.

TINA

It gets worse.

JAMIE

It does.

SHELLY
(Sobbing)
He says I'm a fat little pig who isn't good enough to
lick his feet.

TINA
And "P.S. But if you still want to meet out in the
church tool shed, I wouldn't mind."

SAM
Oh, come on. What a jerk?

JAMIE
He really wrote that after what he said.

SHELLY
I thought he loved me.
                    (Runs inside house)

JAMIE
Shouldn't someone go talk to her?

SAM
No, leave her alone.

TINA
Ma will probably talk to her. Meanwhile I'll be thinking
of a way to get back at Fred.

MA
(Comes out)
What's wrong with, Shelly? She ran upstairs and
locked herself in the bathroom.

TINA
Some guy from church wrote her a nasty letter.

MA
Poor thing. Was it really bad?

SAM
Let's just say if Shelly killed him, I would understand.

MA
That bad? I'll go talk to her.

                              TINA
Let me, Ma. Sometimes I can cheer her up.

                               MA
Okay, Tina. Thank you.
                    (TINA exits inside)
I hope Shelly doesn't get worked up over this?

                              SAM
It doesn't take much.

                               MA
I know, that's what worries me.

                             JAMIE
What are you talking about?

                               MA
Nothing, Jamie. I'll be fine.

                            JIMMY
                         (Enters L)
Hey, Sam, Jamie.
                       (Big smile)
Howdy, Ma.

                               MA
What do you need, Jimmy?

                            JIMMY
I was just being neighborly.

MA
Well, don't be neighborly too long. I need Sam inside
pretty soon.

                              SAM
What for?

                               MA
Peeling potatoes.

                              SAM
                         (Whining)
Aw, Ma.

MA

I don't want to hear it, Sam.
(Looks at watch)
Five minutes.

SAM

Yes, warden.
(MA exits)

JAMIE

I guess I better leave you two alone.

SAM

Thanks.
(JAMIE goes inside)
Howdy, sailor.

JIMMY

Now about my kiss.

(JIMMY tries to kiss SAM but SARGE enters R. SAM pushes JIMMY away. SARGE sits in a chair on the porch. Silence)

SARGE

Don't let me bother you. I'm just gonna do a little reading.
(Looks at a magazine)

JIMMY
Well, I guess I'll be going.

SAM

But our five minutes aren't up yet.

(SARGE looks over the edge of the magazine)

JIMMY
Yeah, but I can't do what I really want to do.

SAM

Can't we just talk?

JIMMY
That's no fun.
(Turns to go)
I'll see you later, Sam.

(JIMMY exits L)

SAM

Bye.

(Heads for house)

SARGE

That boy is a lot like I was when I was his age.

SAM

Really?

SARGE

I'm not sure that's good, Sam. There was only one thing I was interested in when it came to girls and it wasn't talking. I was a real waste of food.

SAM

But you turned out good.

SARGE

Yeah, but not before doing a lot of things I wish I hadn't.

SAM

Like what?

SARGE

Gambling, drinking, womanizing. And I'm not real proud of it either.

SAM

Oh, boys will be boys.

SARGE

And somebody shouldn't let them be. Boys get away with too much nowadays and kids like Jimmy love every minute of it. He don't see it now but it ain't worth it. You hurt too many people along the way.

                    SAM
Jimmy's not that bad, is he?

                    SARGE
I don't know, Sam, is he?

                    SAM
I think he's okay.

                    SARGE
You be careful, Sam.

                    SAM
I can take care of myself, Sarge. Nothing bad's gonna
happen to me.

                    SARGE
Promise?

                    SAM
Don't you always say never make promises?

                    SARGE
Only ones you can't keep.

                    SAM
Well, I think I can keep this one.

                    SARGE
Good.

                    TINA
                  (Runs out)
SARGE!

                    SARGE
What is it?

                    TINA
Shelly's tried to kill herself again!

                    SARGE
                  (Jumps up)
Where is she?

                              TINA
Upstairs. In the bathroom. She cut her wrists. She's
bleeding real bad.

                             SARGE
Go get the truck started. I'll bring her down.

(TINA exits L and SARGE goes inside. JAMIE comes out really upset)

                             JAMIE
Sam. Did you hear?

                              SAM
                          (Disgusted)
Yeah, I heard. What's new?

                             JAMIE
What are you saying? Shelly tried to kill herself...

                              SAM
...for the hundredth time. She does it all the time,
Jamie. It's no big thrill for me.

                             JAMIE
But... this is serious... how can you not care...

                              SAM
Sometimes people get tired of caring!

(PAULA and MA come out)

                              MA

Paula. Go call the EMT in town and have her meet us
at the gas station. Tell her to have an ambulance sent
up too.

                             PAULA
Yes, Ma.
                        (Runs back inside)

                             TINA
                          (Enters L)
The truck's ready.

(SARGE carries her out. Shelly's wrists are expertly wrapped. Shelly cries out despite being weak)

                              SHELLY
              No, leave me alone!

                              SARGE
                              (Kindly)
              Quiet down, Shelly.

                              SHELLY
                              (Struggles)
              No!

                              MA
                              (Goes to SHELLY)
              Shelly, please don't fight.

(SARGE is having trouble holding SHELLY)

                              SHELLY
              I don't want Sarge! Pig!

                              MA
              Shelly!

                              SHELLY
              All you men are pigs!

                              MA
              Stop fighting!

                              SHELLY
              No!

                              SARGE
              Shelly, please. I'll only carry you to the truck.

                              SHELLY
              Then only Ma. Please.

                              SARGE
              Yes, Shelly. Only Ma.

(Carries her off L. MA follows. TINA, SAM, and JAMIE stand silent a moment as car door slams and truck speeds away)

JAMIE
(After a moment)
Will she be okay?

TINA
She didn't cut herself too bad this time. I bet she'll still
have to go to the hospital though.

JAMIE
Why didn't they have the ambulance come here?

TINA
The nearest ambulance is 70 miles away. The EMT in
town is the best person to go to for now.

JAMIE
(Looks off L)
Man, look at Uncle Joe. He looks really upset.

SAM
That's probably why Shelly does it.

TINA
Shut up, Sam. You don't know what you're talking
about.

SAM
What's the matter? Did I insult your girlfriend?

TINA
(Pushes Sam)
You wanna fight.
(Pushes again)
I'll fight you.

(SAM tackles TINA and they fight)

JAMIE
Sarge!

SARGE
(Runs in and grabs them)
All right, break it up!
(Pushes them apart)
Okay, who started it?

                    (They're silent)
Sam, go upstairs.

                    SAM
What? Why only me?

                    SARGE
Don't argue with me, Sam.

                    SAM
She did it too.

                    SARGE
I'll take care of it. Now march!
          (SAM is almost in tears. She runs inside)
Tina, out to the barn.

                    TINA
You're not gonna whip me, are you?

                    SARGE
                    (Tired)
I don't know yet. Get.

(TINA goes. Silence. JAMIE feels awkward. SARGE sighs and grabs his
headphones from the porch and goes DR. He almost collapses at the flower
bed. He sits there motionless. JAMIE doesn't know what to do. Lights fade to
black)

                    END OF ACT I

ACT II

Scene 1

(Lights come up on the same scene as Act I. The only change is SARGE's garden, which is showing some signs of life. Whether the life is weed or flower is unknown. It is very early morning but
the moon is full and the scene is well lit [though the lighting is distinctly different]. As the scene opens, JIMMY comes stumbling on drunk. He drags on a ladder that he puts against the cover
over the porch [if an upstairs is not used then Jimmy will go to a front window instead of an upstairs window]. JIMMY climbs the ladder and talks speaking as he approaches SAM's bedroom window)

JIMMY

Where's my sweet little chicky? She's gone and I'm all alone. Like Rodeo and Juliet, split up by their ma and pa, left with aching hearts. I got an achky-breaky heart baby and I'm coming for you.
                    (Knocks on window)
I can hear you now. "Oh, Rodeo. Oh, Rodeo. Where fartest you, Rodeo."
                    (Laughs at his own joke)
Oh, Juliet.
                    (Knocks)
Juliet! If you don't come out, you gonna see yonder window break.

JAMIE

(Opens window. She is sleepy and cranky)
What do you want?

JIMMY

Can Sam come out and play?

JAMIE

She's asleep like I was before you started banging on our window.

                    JIMMY
Can't you wake her up?

                    JAMIE
No!

(SAM slams window down on his finger)

                    JIMMY
OW!
                (Sucks on his finger)

                    SAM
                (Sleepily. Off)
Who's out there, Jamie?

                    JAMIE
A sick loon.

                    SAM
                (Opens window)
Jimmy?

                    JIMMY
Oh, hi, Sam. Gosh you look perdy.

                    SAM
What are you doing out there? You're gonna get me
in trouble.

                    JIMMY
I need you, Sam. I'm feeling lonely.

                    SAM
You've been drinking. You know I don't like you when
you're drunk.

                    JIMMY
Oh, come on, Sam. I've got needs you know.

                         SAM
So do I and I need sleep… go away.

                         JIMMY
I ain't leaving.

                         SAM
Well, I ain't coming.

                         JIMMY
I feel my heart about to break.
                    (He falls against wall of house near the
                    window and starts a sick howl)
Owoooo!

                         SAM
                    (Falls half out of window to cover his
                    mouth)
Stop that! You'll wake Sarge.

                         JIMMY
                    (Pulls her out)
I got you.

                         SAM
                    (Pushes him)
Quit playing around.

                         JIMMY
                    (Rolls near edge)
Look out below.
                    (SAM grabs him)
You do care.
                    (Throws his arms around her)

                         SAM
                    (Pulls away)
Stop it.

                         JIMMY
Why are you being so mean?

                         SAM
Me?

                         JIMMY

I just want a little love.

SAM

What you need is a cold shower and some coffee.

JIMMY

You're what I need, Sam. Don't you need me?

SAM

What I need is a big club.

JIMMY

But Sam. I'm hurting inside. Don't you care?

SAM

Not when you're like this.

JIMMY
(Angry)

Fine. I'll go.
(Goes to ladder)
Give me my ring.

SAM

What?

JIMMY

Give me my ring.

SAM

You don't mean it.

JIMMY

If you don't want me around, then I don't want
you. Give it!
(SAM sadly takes off ring)

SAM
(Gets a mischievous look)

Fetch boy.

(She throws it off R)

JIMMY

Oh, man.

(JIMMY gets down and runs off R)

                              JAMIE
                       (Pokes her head out)
          Is he gone?

                              SAM
                           (Sad)
          Uh-huh.

                              JAMIE
          Are you okay?

                              SAM
                    (Sits and rubs her finger)
          No.
                          (Holds out hand)
          I gave him back his ring.

                              JAMIE
          You did?

(JAMIE crawls out)

                              SAM
          Maybe I should have gone with him.

                              JAMIE
          But he was so drunk. He smelled like a sick skunk.

                              SAM
          Oh, he always smells like that.
                          (They laugh a little)
          I really love him, Jamie, but sometimes... sometimes
          he can be such a creep.

                              JAMIE
          There's a lot better guys in the world. Once you get
          out of here, you'll see that.

                              SAM
          But that's just it, Jamie. All the guys I've met are
          creeps. I attract them like flies to manure.

                              JAMIE
          Don't say that. You're a lot better than manure.

                    SAM

Thanks, I think.

                    JAMIE

That didn't come out right.

                    SAM

Let's not worry about it. We have other pressing
matters to deal with.

                    JAMIE

What's that?

                    SAM

Sarge's letter.

(SAM takes it out)

                    JAMIE

You kept it?

                    SAM

Sarge won't miss it.

                    JAMIE

But it isn't yours.

                    SAM

Now you sound like, Paula. Fine Miss Prissy Pants. I'll
read it on my own.

(SAM opens letter)

                    JAMIE

Since you opened it, I might as well listen.

                    SAM
                  (Smiles)

Sure. Why not?
                  (Reads)

"Dear Miyo, Thank you for sending me a picture of
Little Billy. He is growing up fast. I see he is wearing
the baseball cap I sent him. I hope he grows up to be
a great baseball player like his father."

JAMIE
Now I know we shouldn't be reading this.

SAM
I knew Sarge did some things he doesn't like to talk about but this... this is too good.

JAMIE
If we get caught with this letter...

SAM
(Excited)
It gets better.
(Reads)
"If you ever need any more money, just ask. I have some money set aside that Betty doesn't know about."
(Aside)
The plot thickens. It looks like Sarge was doing more than fighting in Vietnam. And if this is something Ma doesn't even know about... Wow. In the wrong hands, this letter could be a powerful tool to be used against Sarge.

(SAM has a devious look on her face. The sun is coming up)

JAMIE
I say we get rid of it before we get into trouble.

SAM
Then go back to bed, 'cause I'm readin' it.

JAMIE
That letter's private.

SAM
I said you didn't have to listen.

JAMIE
I know, but what about Sarge?

SAM
What about him?

JAMIE
He wouldn't want us reading it.

SAM

He'll never know. We won't get caught.

(Door opens below)

JAMIE

What was that?

SAM

Get down.

(They hide as PAULA comes out)

SAM (CONT.)

It's only, Paula.

PAULA

What a beautiful morning. Oh thank you, God for making sure I didn't miss this.

SAM

I hate morning people.

JAMIE

Shh!

PAULA

Look at that sun rising out of the mountains. You know, I think I'm getting a little peek at God.
                    (Rooster crows)
Oh, I'm coming Colonel Sanders. I haven't forgotten about you.
                    (Exits R)

SAM

That girl is so weird.

JAMIE

I wish I could be that happy in the morning. The only thing I like to see this early is my pillow.

SARGE
(Appears at window)
There you are. What are you girls doing?

(SAM stuffs letter down JAMIE's shirt and turns with a smile to face SARGE)

                        SAM
          We got up early to see the sunset.

                        JAMIE
          Sunrise.

                        SAM
          Sunrise. I've been bragging to Jamie so much about it
          she just had to see it.

                        SARGE
          And how would you know how nice they are? You're
          never up this early.

                        SAM
          How would you know?

                        SARGE
          Because I'm always up this early.

                        SAM
          Oh.

                        SARGE
          A ladder? How did that get there?

                        SAM
          A ladder? Gee I don't know. Did you know there was
          a ladder there Jamie?

                        JAMIE
          Come on, Sam. I'm tired. Let's go back to bed.

                        SARGE
          Sounds like a good idea to me.

(SARGE goes inside window)

                        SAM
          That was a close one.

                        JAMIE
          Yeah, Sarge was sleeping pretty hard there wasn't
          he?

SAM
How was I supposed to know he got up this early?
(Reaches for the letter)
Where's the letter?

JAMIE
I don't think we should read it, Sam.

SAM
Hand it over or you'll be sorry.

JAMIE
Looks like I'll be sorry either way.

(JAMIE hands over letter)

SAM
Thanks.
(JAMIE heads back inside)
Don't you want to hear it?

JAMIE
Not really.

SAM
Oh, come on. What are you, chicken?

JAMIE
No, tired. Goodnight, Sam.
(JAMIE goes inside)

SAM
Gee whiz.
(Looks at letter)
Now it's no fun.

SARGE
(Appears below [or at door])
Sam?!
(SAM stuffs letter in her shirt)

SAM
What is this, a prison camp? Can't a person have a
few moments to herself?

SARGE

Get back inside.

SAM

But Sarge...

SARGE

Back inside now or I might decide to find out the real reason you're up so early.

(SAM looks worried and heads for window)

PAULA
(Rushes on from R upset)
Sarge. You got to go to the barn quick.

(SAM stops)

SARGE

What is it, Paula?

PAULA

It's Jimmy. He's in the barn... naked.

SARGE

Naked?

PAULA

He's up in the hay loft, swing around, saying he's Tarzan. And he's naked...

SARGE

I'll go take care of it.

SAM
(Excited)
I'll go with you.

SARGE

You get in your room and don't come out until I tell you. Now I know why you were up so early. Things are starting to become clear to me now.

(SARGE runs off R. SAM waves letter when he's gone)

SAM
You're not the only one who knows something, Sarge.

(She exits inside and PAULA sits on steps upset)

JAMIE
Paula? Are you okay?

PAULA
(Sobbing)
Yes, I'm fine.

JAMIE
Did something happen, Paula?

PAULA
Jimmy's naked.

(She covers her face and cries)

JAMIE
He's what?!

PAULA
Naked. He's in the barn swinging around. He thinks he's Tarzan.

JAMIE

(Trying not to laugh)
Oh.

PAULA
It was awful.

JAMIE
I'll bet it was.

PAULA
(Pause. Grows quieter)
I've never seen a boy naked before.

JAMIE
(Gets a disgusted look on her face)
And Jimmy was the first.

PAULA

What do you think about Jimmy?

JAMIE

Jimmy?

PAULA

Yeah. You think he's okay?

JAMIE

Well, let's just say if he and I were Adam and Eve, I'd probably do the world a favor and not reproduce.

PAULA

So you don't like him?

JAMIE

Let's just say he's not my type.

PAULA

Oh.
                    (Looks upset)

JAMIE

Why do you ask?

PAULA

Well, Jimmy was saying all kinds of stuff to me in there. Stuff I've never thought of before and well... I kind of liked some of it.

JAMIE

Oh.

PAULA

You know, I've never even been on a date. I mean being single was fine for Jesus and all, but I got special needs. Is that bad of me to think that way?

JAMIE

Well, no...

PAULA

I'd really like to get to know a boy. Hold his hand.
                    (Embarrassed)
Kiss him...

JAMIE

I don't think Jimmy's quite what you have in mind.

PAULA

I guess not, but there really isn't anybody else.

JAMIE

You go to church don't you?

PAULA

Yeah.

JAMIE

Don't you like any guys there?

PAULA

They all think I'm weird. Heck, they think all of us are weird. The only one of us they'll have anything to do with is Shelly and we all know why they like her.

JAMIE

Why's that?

PAULA

'Cause she's pretty.

JAMIE

You're pretty.

PAULA

Not like that.

JAMIE

No, but in your own special way.

PAULA

But guys don't want special.

JAMIE

Some do.

PAULA

I haven't met any.

JAMIE

One will come along.

PAULA

You think so?

JAMIE

Sure.
(PAULA smiles)
Tell you what. Why don't we go up to your room and I'll show you just how pretty you are. We'll put some make-up on you, do your hair, and find a dress that compliments your better qualities.

PAULA

I don't know.

JAMIE

Come on. It'll be fun. And if you don't like it, you can wash it all off.

PAULA
(Smiles)

Jamie?

JAMIE

Yeah?

PAULA

Why are you being so nice to me?

JAMIE

What do you mean?

PAULA

Nobody else here cares. At least not any of the girls.

JAMIE

I'll have to tell you, Paula. Not everybody is like the girls you live with here. There are some pretty nice people out there. Sometimes they're hard to find, but they're there.

PAULA

I'm sure glad I found one of them.

JAMIE

I am too. Let's go.

(They go inside arm in arm. SARGE and JIMMY enter R. JIMMY is mostly dressed. SARGE points at the steps on the porch)

SARGE

Sit.

(JIMMY does. SARGE stares at JIMMY a minute)

JIMMY

Are you gonna kill me, Sarge?

SARGE

I'm thinking about it.
            (Pause. JIMMY is very nervous)
What were you doing up there? And don't lie to me. I was once a pretty good liar myself, so I know one when I see one.

JIMMY

I guess I had a little too much to drink.

SARGE

Right under your parent's noses...

JIMMY

Man, they don't care. You should see them sometime. Talk about drunk.

SARGE

But you're just a kid.

JIMMY

I'm almost 18. And I only have two years of high school left.

SARGE

You may not make it to 18 if you keep this up.
            (JIMMY gets quiet)
What else were you doing over here?

JIMMY

I was looking for Sam.

                    SARGE

I thought so.

                    JIMMY

Then why'd you ask?

                    SARGE

Don't get mouthy.

                    JIMMY

Sorry. It's the booze talking.

                    SARGE

Well, it better stop talking or it's going to get dunked
into the water trough.

                    JIMMY

We didn't do nothing, Sarge. Sam kicked me out
even.

                    SARGE

She did?

                    JIMMY

She didn't want to get in trouble. Man, was she mean
to me.

                    SARGE

She was?

                    JIMMY

I was so mad at her for not coming. That's why I did
the Tarzan bit in the barn. I wanted you to think there
was more going on.

                    SARGE

Was there?

                    JIMMY

No! Sam and I didn't do nothing. Really.
                    (Mad)
All we did was fight. I made her give my ring back.

                    SARGE

The promise ring?

JIMMY

Yeah. But she threw it somewhere. Now I can't find it.

SARGE

It's right here.
                    (Takes it out of pocket)
I found it on the way to the barn.

JIMMY

Maybe it's a sign. Maybe Sam and me is supposed to make up.

SARGE

Maybe so. Maybe not.
                    (Pause)
I'm not sure I want you around Sam anymore.

JIMMY

Oh.

SARGE

But she really likes you and if she wanted to be with you she'd find a way.
                    (Paces)
The more I'd say no, the more she'd find times to sneak away.
                    (Studies JIMMY)
So maybe we can take care of this some other way.

JIMMY
                    (Nervous)
Uh... like how?

SARGE

Growing up, I did a lot of stupid things too. Maybe not as crazy as Tarzan, but I was wild. See my mother died when I was real young and my pappy didn't want to take care of me. So my family sent me around, hoping somebody could handle me, but I only got worse. My big moment was in a barn too. But I burnt it down. That's when my Aunt Minnie took me in. And for the first time somebody loved me no matter what I did wrong. Even though I didn't change overnight, that love stuck with me. And as I grew older, that love become more and more a part of me until all the hate was gone.

JIMMY

So what's your point?

SARGE

The point is, Jimmy, that you need some love. Not the kind of love that involves sex, but a caring kind of love.
(Pause)
And maybe Sam can give that to you.

JIMMY

I don't think she wants to now.

SARGE

Maybe she will. Let's bring her out and give it a try.

JIMMY

I don't know. I was a real jerk last night.

SARGE

If you're not ready then we shouldn't do it. You have to want to change.

JIMMY

I want to. I always want to, but it's hard. Wasn't it hard for you?

SARGE

It took more than 30 years.

JIMMY

Thirty years?

SARGE

More probably. I stopped counting.
(Frowns at the memories)
I used to have some awful habits. Drinking, smoking,
gambling. Gambling was the worst. I gave up the
other things with no problem, but gambling... I still
can't even look at a deck of cards.

JIMMY

How did you finally give it up?

SARGE

I don't know that I have. A few years ago I was caught
up in it again. Some old friend invited me over and
they thought what I'd love was a game of poker cause
that's what we used to do together. Of course they
talked me into playing. What a terrible night.

JIMMY

You lost big, huh?

SARGE

No, I won.

JIMMY

How much?

SARGE

Several hundred dollars.

JIMMY

Really? Cool.

SARGE

No, it wasn't. I felt the old desires coming back. I was
secretly planning a trip to Nevada in my head. I never
did spend any of the money though. I couldn't.

JIMMY

Do you still have it?

                    SARGE
No. I felt too guilty I did the only thing I could think of
to make up for it.

                    JIMMY
What?

                    SARGE
I gave it to our church.

                    JIMMY
All of it?

                    SARGE
All of it.

                    JIMMY
Too bad.

                    SARGE
So are you willing to give something up for Sam?

                    JIMMY
Like what?

                    SARGE
Drinking maybe.

                    JIMMY
But all my friends drink.

                    SARGE
You need different friends.

                    JIMMY
Everyone will think I'm a total loser.

                    SARGE
Sam won't.

                    JIMMY
                (Sighs. Looks at ring)
I guess I could give it a try.

                    SARGE
No. Either you will or you won't. There's no in middle
or maybe.

                    JIMMY
                    (Thinks)
Okay. I will. For Sam.

                    SARGE
I'll get her.
                    (Opens door)
Sam. Will you come down please?
(SAM steps out)

                    JIMMY
                    (Stands. Paces)
What should I say to her?

                    SARGE
Whatever you feel is right.

                    SAM
                    (Comes out)
Yeah, Sarge.
                    (Sees JIMMY)
What's he doing here?

                    SARGE
I had a little talk with him. Now I think it's your turn.

(SARGE sits on porch and pretend to read a magazine. He keeps
watch on the following. Long pause. SAM is staring at JIMMY with
a mean look. Finally she speaks)

                    SAM
Well?

                    JIMMY
I'm sorry.

                    SAM
If you are so sorry, why do you keep doing it? This
isn't the first time you've come around at night acting
like a baboon.

JIMMY
I swear, Sam. If you take me back, I'll stop drinking.

SAM
But you'll only stop if I take you back.

JIMMY
No, I'm quitting. I promise.

SAM
(Pause. Studies him)
You really want me back.

JIMMY
More than anything.

(They stare happily at each other. SARGE rolls his eyes)

SARGE
Go ahead and hug him.

(They hug happily)

SAM
Could we go for a walk, Sarge?

SARGE
I guess. But don't go far.

SAM
We won't.

SARGE
And stay out of the barn.
(SAM laughs as they exit L)
I hope this doesn't backfire on me.

(JAMIE comes out)

JAMIE
Ma isn't back with Shelly yet, huh?

SARGE
Nope. But they should be here soon. The doctor gave
the okay last night.

                    JAMIE
Where's Sam?

                    SARGE
Taking a walk with Jimmy.

                    JAMIE
They made up?

                    SARGE
Guess so.

                    JAMIE
And Tina's still in bed.

                    SARGE
Why? What ya' need?

                    JAMIE
I had something I wanted to show everyone.

                    SARGE
What is it?

                    JAMIE
Maybe I should wait for everybody.

                    SARGE
I ain't nobody, you know.

                    JAMIE
Okay. I'll be right back.

(JAMIE disappears inside. SARGE smiles and waits. JAMIE is inside and calls out:)

                    JAMIE (CONT.)
Now close your eyes, Sarge.

                    SARGE
                 (Closing eyes)
Yes, ma'am.

                    JAMIE
Here we come.

(JAMIE comes out with PAULA who is done up beautifully in make-up, a new hair style, and a very nice dress. JAMIE guides her out. PAULA is embarrassed)

                    JAMIE (CONT.)
Okay, Sarge.

                    SARGE
          (Sees PAULA. Is surprised)
Well, look at you.

                    PAULA
Is that good?

                    SARGE
You look wonderful, Paula. I almost didn't recognize you.

                    PAULA
Really?

                    SARGE
You're as pretty as any girl I've ever seen.

                    PAULA
          (Blushing)
Thanks, Sarge.

                    JAMIE
See, Paula. You are pretty.

                    PAULA
I guess so.

                    JAMIE
We need a picture of this.

                    SARGE
You bet we do. I'll go get my camera.
          (Goes inside)

                    PAULA
This is so wonderful. Thank you, Jamie.

                    JAMIE
It was no trouble at all.

JIMMY
(He enters from R with SAM)
Hey, who is this?

JAMIE

Can't you tell?

JIMMY
(Looks hard. PAULA looks away)
Is that...no way. Paula?

JAMIE

Sure is.

JIMMY
You are lookin' fine, Paula. Mighty fine. I didn't know
you were so good-lookin'.

PAULA
Me neither.

JAMIE
It's a shame she's been hiding it all this time.

JIMMY
I don't know where it was, but it sure looks good now.

SAM
(Punches him)
Hey, you watch yourself.

JIMMY
I didn't mean nothing by it.
(SAM goes to door)
I was only trying to make her feel good.

SAM
I have to go make breakfast.
(Exits inside)

PAULA
Sam's making breakfast? I thought she couldn't cook.

JAMIE
Maybe I better go help her.

(Exits inside)

JIMMY

I better go home too. Man, I am going to get it.

PAULA
(Shy)

Bye, Jimmy.

JIMMY
(Smiles)

Bye, Paula. Boy, you are one hot looking chick.

(PAULA is embarrassed but happy. SARGE comes out with camera. TINA follows)

SARGE

Doesn't Paula look great?

TINA
(Laughs)

Yeah. Too bad it isn't Halloween yet.

SARGE

Tina!

PAULA

She's just jealous. Everybody else thinks I look great.
(Goes inside)

SARGE

Now she's upset.

(Exits inside)

TINA

What did I do? Geez. Some people can't take a joke.
(Hears truck)
Well, look who's here. Hi, Ma! Hey, Shelly! Welcome home!

MA
(MA and SHELLY enter L)

Thank you, Tina.

SHELLY

Boy, oh, boy, did I miss your cookin', Ma. I don't know where they get that hospital food, but it ain't from an animal, a vegetable, or a mineral.

TINA

They do that so you don't want to stay.

SHELLY

It worked.

MA

You girls go ahead and talk. I'll take your bag inside.

SHELLY

Thanks, Ma.
(She kisses MA and hugs her. MA takes SHELLY's bag inside. SHELLY and TINA sit on the front porch)

TINA

I'm glad to have you back. I don't think I could have handled these screwballs by myself much longer.

SHELLY

I'm pretty much glad to be back. I'm gonna miss one thing though.

TINA

What's that?

SHELLY

Mr. Lincoln Jefferson Jones.

TINA

Who?

SHELLY

The most gorgeous hunk o' boy my eyes ever feasted on.

TINA

He ain't a doctor is he?

SHELLY

Nope, not yet anyway. Jeffy was a volunteer there.

                    TINA
Jeffy?

                    SHELLY
That's what I called him.

                    TINA
How did you meet him?

                    SHELLY
Jeffy volunteered at the hospital as a service to the
community. He says he's always trying to find ways to
help people.

                    TINA
I know how he could help you.
                    (They laugh)

                    SHELLY
He's so perfect. Straight A's and student body
president.

                    TINA
He ain't a geek?

                    SHELLY
No, honey, he's fine.

                    TINA
So what kind of service did he do for you?

                    SHELLY
We just did a lot of talking.

                    TINA
Yeah, right.

                    SHELLY
                    (Winks)
And maybe a little more.

                    TINA
I knew it.

                              SHELLY
But it all was very proper. 'Cause I'm a proper kind of
girl.

                              TINA
You are?

                              SHELLY
                          (Hits TINA)
When I want to be.

                              TINA
So what did you do?

                              SHELLY
Be patient. One step at a time.

                              TINA
Okay. How did it get started?

                              SHELLY
He was the one that delivered flowers to all the
rooms. I saw him all the time and smiled when he
went by. I guess I did enough smiling, 'cause one day
he stopped with some flowers for me.

                              TINA
Who from?

                              SHELLY
Him.

                              TINA
Score!

                              SHELLY
"They were left over," he said. He thought I might like
some. That's when the talkin' started. I told him my
name was Mercedes Masterson.

                              TINA
You didn't.

                              SHELLY
I did. He called me Mercy for short.

TINA

Heaven help us.
(They laugh)
What else did you tell him?

SHELLY

I said I was a cheerleader and a tennis champ. I said I
go to a private girls' school in California and I let him
know I sure miss boys out there.

TINA

Go, Shelly, go.

SHELLY
(In a high class voice)
That's Mercy, dear.

TINA

Is that how you talked?

SHELLY

Of course, dear.
(Laughs, back to normal voice)
It drove him wild.

TINA

What else did you tell him?

SHELLY

That I was very lost and confused and I needed some
guidance. My mum and my dad were never around
and I really needed someone to help me.

TINA

This is better than TV.

SHELLY

He wanted to help so bad. He was a sweetie.

TINA

Is this where the kissing comes in?

SHELLY

Mercy looks for the finer qualities in men.

TINA

Yeah, right.

SHELLY

He knew I was leaving so he snuck in last night.

TINA

Yeah?

SHELLY

It was nice.

TINA

That's all?

SHELLY

What more do you want? You want me to tell it to you blow by blow?

TINA

Why not?

SHELLY

Forget it. There are some things we never tell.

TINA

Since when?

SHELLY

Since I met Jeffy.

TINA

Did you get his number?

SHELLY

Yeah.

TINA

Did he ask for yours?

SHELLY

Yeah, but I told him mummy would be furious. Mummy wants me to marry someone that's really, really rich. But I said I couldn't stand all those rich jerks. But if I don't marry one, I lose all of my money. And you know what he said?

                    TINA
What?

                    SHELLY
"Money doesn't matter, only you."

                    TINA
This is too good to be true.

                    SHELLY
                    (Smiles)
I know.

                    TINA
Are you going to call him?

                    SHELLY
I don't know if I should.

                    TINA
Why not?

                    SHELLY
It was fun at the time, but I don't...

                    TINA
You got a hot one. Don't lose him now.

                    SHELLY
We'll see.

                    TINA
You're crazy to let this one go.

                    SHELLY
I guess.

(SARGE enters from inside)

                    TINA
Hey, Sarge. Looks who's back.

                    SARGE
Hi, Shelly. How you doing?

SHELLY

Okay.

TINA

Sounds like she's doing great to me.

SHELLY
(Playfully)

Oh, you be quiet.

SARGE

Hey, look at that smile. That's what I like to see.

SHELLY

Sorry I was so mean when you were carrying me.

SARGE

Don't worry about it.

SHELLY

I know sometimes we don't get along, but that was
pretty bad.

SARGE

I said don't worry...

SHELLY

Man, can't I even apologize? I'm trying to be nice here
and you won't even let me.

SARGE

Let's not argue...

SHELLY

I'm not arguing.

SARGE

I didn't say you were.

SHELLY

You did too.

TINA
(Trying to avoid a conflict)

Hey, Shelly. Why don't we go for a walk?

                          SHELLY
Sure, why don't we?
                          (They start to go)

                          PAULA
                          (Runs out)
FIRE!

                          SHELLY
                          (She and TINA return)
What?

                          PAULA
                          (Stops. Smiles pleasantly)
Oh, hi, Shelly.

                          SARGE
Paula! What fire?

                          PAULA
                          (Remembers. Gets upset)
Sam started a fire.

(SAM and JAMIE run out)

                          SAM
                          (Excited)
Did you see that?!
                          (Makes explosion sound)
Foooom!

                          JAMIE
                          (Sarcastic)
Yeah, Sam, it was great.

                          SARGE
Where's Ma?

                          JAMIE
                          (Worried)
I don't know.

(MA appears and is black from the smoke)

                          SARGE
Are you okay?

                              MA
Yes.

                    (They are try not to laugh, but it's hard
                         not to. MA does look funny)
Sam?

                             SAM
                    (Trying not to laugh)
Yes?

                              MA
Is it okay if I make breakfast?

                             SAM
Sure, Ma.

                              MA
Thank you.

(MA exits inside)

                            PAULA
                    (To TINA and SHELLY)
You've gotta see this.

(PAULA, TINA, and SHELLY rush inside)

                            JAMIE
I told you not to flip the bacon.

                             SAM
Okay, so I made a mistake. So sue me.

                            SARGE
Why don't we go in and help Ma clean up?

(SARGE goes in)

                             SAM
I don't think Ma really wants to see me right now.

                            JAMIE
Come on.

(They exit inside. Lights fade to black)

ACT 2

Scene 2

(Lights come up on SAM and SARGE. SARGE is working on his garden and SAM does not look like she is in a good mood. SAM walks cautiously up to SARGE)

                            SAM
Sarge?

                            SARGE
Yes, ma'am?

                            SAM
Have you ever done something you wish you hadn't done?

                            SARGE
                        (Laughs)
More than I care to remember.

                            SAM
I wish I couldn't remember this last one.

                            SARGE
Why? What happened?

                            SAM
                (Wants to tell, but doesn't)
I'm just in trouble with Ma over something. That's all.

(She turns away. JAMIE comes out. SARGE stands)

                            SARGE
It will all come out in the wash.
                (Stops himself from saying more)
But I guess I'd better stay out of it. If you'll excuse me. I've got to check on the ladies.

                            JAMIE
The ladies?

                            SAM
He means the cows.

JAMIE

Oh.

(SARGE exits R. SAM sits on the steps, upset)

JAMIE (CONT.)

What's with you?

SAM

You know that letter, the one Sarge wrote?

JAMIE

Yeah?

SAM

Ma caught me with it.

JAMIE
(Sits)

Oh, dear.

SAM

Yeah. She was so mad she made me wait out here
until she decided what to do with me.
(Upset)
I watched her read the letter too. I think she started to
cry.

JAMIE

What did the rest of the letter say?

SAM

It had more stuff about the kid. I think that lady wants
to send him to America to live with Sarge. Ma would
love that.

JAMIE

I wonder what Ma's gonna do.

SAM

I wouldn't be surprised if she killed both me and
Sarge. She's pretty upset.

(Stands. Tears are coming. She can barely be heard)

SAM (CONT.)
Why do I always do this?

JAMIE
(Goes to her)
Do what?

SAM
Mess things up.
(Pause)
I get something good then I mess it up.
(Kicks something handy)
I always have to go and spoil things for people. I just try to have a little fun... but... I don't know when to stop. I keep playing... like a little kid who tells a funny joke over and over. They keep saying it 'cause it was funny once so it should be funny a bunch of times. Then when it's not funny anymore, they don't know how to quit. They keep trying, hoping it will still be funny. They keep on joking until someone gets mad and... hurts you.
(Pause)
I'm always playing games. I can't stop.
(She has trouble speaking)
I... can't... stop.
(JAMIE wants to say something but doesn't know what. MA appears at screen door. Girls don't see MA. SAM gains control again)

SAM (CONT.)
I always hurt someone. My daddy left because of me.
(Sees JAMIE's reaction)
He did. I found a letter he wrote my mama. He said he didn't want to be tied down by a kid.
(Chokes)
Mama said it was for the best.
(Sad)
But I ran Mama off too. She had better things to do than to sit around playing my games.
(Looks at house)
And I'm still playing my little games. I should have listened to you, Jamie. You got a good head. You stopped playing games when you were two or three I bet. Adults always like you... Me? I get 'em to like to hate me. Get 'em so worked up they want nothing but to have me gone.

JAMIE
(After long pause)
Oh, Sam. I'm sorry.

SAM
(Laughs over crying)
Sorry? Don't be sorry. You gotta admit, I do it well.

JAMIE
Don't be so hard on yourself, Sam. You're a good person. People like you.

SAM

Just drop it, Jamie.
(Sits. Trying to control her crying)
I'm sure you've got better things to do.
(JAMIE doesn't know what to do. SAM looks away)

SAM (CONT.)
I wanna be alone.

(JAMIE nods and exit R)

MA
(Comes out)
Sam. Can we talk now?
(SAM is silent)
I can't lie and say I'm not angry. What you did wasn't very nice. Something like this can hurt a lot of people. It could hurt me, it could hurt Sarge, and it could hurt you.
(MA sits by SAM)
But it doesn't mean I don't love you anymore.

SAM
(Gets up)
Why do you have to talk so much?
(Turns. Angry)
Can't you get it over with! Can't you punish me and be done with it!
(Turns away)
I hate all this talk. Doesn't get us anywhere.

MA

Sam. I think you've punished yourself more than I ever could. But there is one thing I want you to do. I want you to tell Sarge what you did.

SAM

I... I can't.

MA

You have to learn to face your troubles, Sam. I can't always be around to clean up after you.

SAM

Sarge will hate me.

MA

He won't hate you, Sam. None of us hate you.

SAM

But I'm so awful.

MA

There's nothing you could do that would make us stop loving you. We might be angry, we might yell and scream, but we'd never stop loving you.

SAM
(Sighs)

Okay. I'll tell him.

MA

Good.

SAM

But if he never talks to me again, it'll be all your fault.

MA
(Tries to hide her smile)
That's a chance I'll just have to take.

(MA exits. SAM paces, wondering what to say to SARGE)

JAMIE
(Returns)
I saw Ma leave. How did it go?

                    SAM
Okay, I guess.

                   JAMIE
What did she say?

                    SAM
She said I have to tell Sarge about what I did.

                   JAMIE
You have to tell him about the letter?

                    SAM
I don't know what to say.
          (JAMIE doesn't either)
Maybe I should go throw myself off a cliff now and
save Sarge the trouble.

                   JAMIE
                 (Shocked)
Sam?!

                    SAM
                 (Smiles)
Oh, don't get your panties in a bunch. I wouldn't really
do it.

                   JAMIE
You never know.

                    SAM
Life ain't that bad.

                   SARGE
              (Returns from R)
Man alive, it is a beautiful day, isn't it?
              (Looks at SAM)
Still under the weather, aye Sammy?

                    SAM
I guess.

(SAM can't bring herself to say anything more)

                              SARGE
Boy, there are too many Gloomy Gusses today. You
ain't too happy and Ma is sure in a mood. I wonder
what's buggin' her?
              (SAM and JAMIE give each other a look)
It can't be the weather. Maybe it's a full moon.
                    (Turns to JAMIE)
How about giving me a helpin' hand, Jamie?

                              JAMIE
What are we doing?

                              SARGE
We're getting a new calf from town and I need some
help bringing the thing here.

                              JAMIE
I think I can handle that.

                              SARGE
It'll be fun. Trust me.
                    (SAM looks away)
Meet me out in the barn. We need to get a few things
first.

(SARGE exits R)

                              JAMIE
When are you going to tell him?

SAM
I don't know. Never I guess.

                              JAMIE
You have to tell him some time.

                               SAM
                            (Annoyed)
That's not really any of your business, now is it?

                              JAMIE
Okay, sorry.

(JAMIE starts to leave but MA comes out with something strange. JAMIE
stays to see what's up)

MA

Sam. Do you know anything about this?

(MA holds up a box from a home pregnancy test)

JAMIE

What is it?

MA

It's a home pregnancy test.

SAM
(Jumps up when she sees it)

It ain't mine.

MA

I want the truth now.

SAM
(Intensely)

But it isn't. I swear.

MA
(Rings breakfast bell)

This has not been my day.

(SHELLY and TINA come running in first)

TINA

Breakfast already?

MA

No, we need to talk.

SHELLY

What about?

MA

I'll wait 'til we're all here.

PAULA
(Enters)

I'm starved. Hey, what we all doin' out here?

                    SHELLY
                    (Snotty)
    We all gotta talk.

(SARGE comes last)

                    SARGE
    It's a little early for breakfast isn't it?

(MA shows the home pregnancy test box)

                    MA
    We have something we need to talk about.
    I found this in the bathroom. I don't normally go
    digging through the garbage, but this caught my eye
    as I was emptying the trash.

                    SHELLY
    It ain't mine.

                    TINA
    No way.

                    PAULA
    Me neither.

                    SHELLY
                    (Evil smile)
    Is it Sam's?

                    SAM
    No.

                    SHELLY
    I bet it is.

                    SAM
    It's yours isn't it, Shelly?

                    SHELLY
    No.

(TINA looks at SHELLY unsure)

                    SAM
    What about Jeffy?

                    SHELLY
How did you know about him?

                    SAM
You have "I love Jeffy" written all over everything.

                    SHELLY
Then there's you and Jimmy.

                    MA
That's enough girls.

                    SHELLY
But that's not mine.

                    SAM
Me neither.

                    MA
Tina and Paula, you can go. I want to talk to Sam and
Shelly.

(PAULA obediently runs in to the house. TINA reluctantly goes
slowly. She wants to hear, but MA gives her a look that hurries her
along)

                    SARGE
You go on too, Jamie. I'll meet you in the barn.

                    JAMIE
Okay.

(JAMIE leaves)

                    MA
I want to talk to Shelly first. Sam, you wait outside.

(MA leads a pouting SHELLY inside)

                    SHELLY
But I didn't do it.

(SAM and SARGE are alone)

                    SARGE
                    (Calmly)
Is it yours, Sam?

                    SAM
                    (Frustrated)
No.

                    SARGE
Are you and Jimmy...?

                    SAM
No!

                    SARGE
Really?

                    SAM
Don't you believe me?

                    SARGE
I do.

                    SAM
I wish Ma would. She always takes Shelly's
side. Shelly will have Ma convinced it was me.

                    SARGE
I only hope whoever it is tells us.

                    SAM
I seriously doubt they will.

                    SARGE
You go ahead and run along. I'll take care of it.

                    SAM
You sure?

                    SARGE
Yeah.

(SAM hugs him)

                         SAM

Thanks.

                         SARGE

No problem.
             (SAM starts to go happily, but stops)
Something wrong?
                      (SAM isn't sure)
You want to talk about something else?

                         SAM

I don't know.

                         SARGE

Is it about Jimmy?

(She isn't sure how to explain the letter)
                         SAM

Well...no.
                         (Pause)
It's about you.

                         SARGE

What?

                         SAM

I found something... something private... that maybe I
shouldn't have seen.

                         SARGE

Something of mine?

                         SAM
                        (Upset)
Yeah.

                         SARGE

What was it?

                         SAM
                        (Pause)
A letter.

                         SARGE

Who was it from?

SAM

It was from you.

SARGE

To whom?

(Pause)

SAM
(Looks away. Grow quiet)
To Vietnam.

SARGE

Oh, man.
(SARGE isn't as upset as
SAM would expect. She's
puzzled by his calmness)
I should be more careful about leaving my letters out
for everyone to see.

(SAM can't bring herself to say any more. MA comes out. SHELLY
is in tears. She exits L)

MA
Your turn Sam.

SARGE

We already talked.

MA
I would like to talk to her too.

SARGE
Sam, why don't you go inside?
(SAM obeys)
It's not her's.

MA
How do you know?

SARGE

I just do.

MA
You do, huh?

SARGE

Look, Betty. Sam and I have an understanding. We
don't keep secrets and we don't lie.

MA

You don't, huh? Then I guess she hasn't told you yet
about her bad habit of reading your letters.

SARGE

How do you know about that?

MA

I caught Sam reading your letter.
                    (Pause)
Sam told you then?

SARGE

Just now.

(MA is surprised. Her expression changes from anger to hurt)

MA

Who is she?

SARGE

Huh? Oh, you mean the letter. I wish I could
remember what the letter said.

(MA pulls it out from her pocket and hands it to SARGE)

MA

I took it from Sam.

SARGE
                    (Looks at envelope)
Return to sender.
                    (Upset)
I hope nothing happened to them.

MA
                    (Mad)
Who are they?

(He looks at MA, unsure about what to say)

SARGE

I wasn't supposed to tell you.

MA

I think you'd better now.

SARGE
(Paces)

Billy didn't want me to tell.

MA
(Shocked)

Billy?

SARGE

Yes, your brother.

MA

Then it's not your...

SARGE
(Laughs)

No.
(Goes to her)

Did you think that the kid was mine?

MA

I didn't know what else to think.

SARGE

Billy met her during the war. She was the only
survivor from her village. Billy was the one who found
her and was the one to take care of her.
(Pause)

Billy wanted to marry her and bring back to the states.
(Pause. SARGE is upset)

But he never made it out.
(MA turns not wanting to
discuss her brother's death)

A lot of good men died over there.

MA

So the boy is Billy's.

SARGE

Yeah.

MA
And you've been helping them?
(SARGE nods)
How come you never told me?

SARGE
I wanted to, but Billy made me promise. I guess he
didn't want his family to be ashamed. They weren't
married yet or anything. It all just sort of happened.
(SARGE looks at letter, confused)
I don't understand why this letter was returned
though. I hope she's okay.

MA
I hope so too.

(MA goes and kisses SARGE)

SARGE
What was that for?

MA
(Smiles)
Can't I kiss you?

SARGE
Why sure, but I...
(Laughs)
Oh, never mind.

(He kisses her back)

MA
I guess I can go then. We'll have to wait out whoever
isn't talking about the pregnancy test. And I said I'd be
there soon.

SARGE
So where is it you're going again?

MA
To help a sick friend.

SARGE

You're keeping something from me, aren't you? This friend wouldn't be a man would it?

MA

It's nothing like that. But it is a secret.

SARGE

I hate secrets.

MA

I know and you can never keep one. That's why I'm not telling you.

SARGE

So the secret doesn't involve me?

MA

No, and that's all I'm telling you.

TINA
(Comes to door)
Can we come out now?

MA

After you get my bags out of my room.

TINA

You're leaving now?

MA

I sure am.

(TINA exits inside)

SARGE

Aren't you going to make breakfast first?

MA

I'll let you handle it.

SARGE

I guess I can do cereal.

MA

You can do more than that? Have one of the girls help you.

(TINA comes out with SHELLY. They are carrying the bags)

TINA

Here they are.

SHELLY

Where do you want them?

(JAMIE, PAULA, and SAM come out)

MA
(To SHELLY and TINA)
Will you take them out to the car?

TINA

No problem.

PAULA
(Worried)
How long you gonna be gone?

MA

As long as it takes my friend to get better.

PAULA

How long is that?

MA
(Smiles and hugs PAULA)
I'll be back soon. You won't even know I'm gone.

SAM
(Joking)
Sarge isn't gonna cook is he?

MA
(Smiles)
I left the number of the hospital by the phone.

SARGE
(Laughs)
I'm not that bad.

                    MA

Shelly and Tina are good cooks.

                    SAM

I hope so.

                    MA

They cook all the time, Sam. Something you need to
start doing soon.

                    SAM

I'm a good cook.

                    SARGE

Toast and microwave popcorn doesn't count.

                    PAULA

Sometimes she even burns those.

                    JAMIE

And remember the last time you tried cooking.

                    SAM

What is this? Pick on Sam day.

                    MA

You all behave while I'm gone. Remember who's in
charge.

                    SAM
                  (Smiles)

Me?

                    MA
                  (Evil eye)

Samantha.

                    SAM
                  (Shivers)

Don't call me that.

                    SARGE

You'd better get going. You want to be there before
dark.

                    MA
I'll call when I get there.

                    JAMIE
Drive safely.

                    PAULA
                    (Sad)
We'll miss you.

                    (Hugs her)

                    SAM
Don't do anything I would do.
                    (MA waves and exits L)
There she goes.

(SHELLY and TINA reenter)

                    SHELLY
It's party time.

                    TINA
The cat's away and we will play.

                    SARGE
You will, huh?

                    SHELLY
Just kidding, Sarge.

                    SARGE
                    (Skeptical)
Uh-huh. You girls got your chores done?

                    TINA
Yeap.

                    SARGE
Mind if I check.

                    SHELLY
Well, maybe not all done. But almost.

                    SARGE
You might as well wait 'til after breakfast.

SHELLY

You want us to cook?

SARGE

No, Sam and I will do it.

SAM

We will?

SARGE

Sure. I did a little cooking in the army.

SAM

Oh, boy. Army food.

SARGE

It's not so bad. My favorite was the raisin
bread. Though I'm still not sure where they got the
raisins from. The guys joked that they were flies that
got stuck in the bread batter. I'm not so sure they
were wrong.

SHELLY

We can cook if you want us to Sarge.

TINA

Hey, yeah, no problem.

SARGE

No, we got it covered, don't we Sammy?

SAM

Uh, yeah, sure.

(SARGE goes happily in. SAM follows looking worried)

TINA

This is going to be scary.
(Motorcycle is heard off L)

SHELLY

Look who's coming?

TINA

If it isn't Sam's knight in shining leather.

                    JIMMY
                    (Off L)
Hi, girls.

                    (Enters)
Got your mail.

                    SHELLY
Thanks, Jimmy.

(SHELLY goes to get it. He pulls it away)

                    JIMMY
What's it worth to you?

(TINA stands. Punches her first into her palm)

                    TINA
What's it worth to you?

(JIMMY hands mail to SHELLY. Speaks to TINA)

                    JIMMY
                    (Annoyed)
Here. I already lost one tooth because of you.

                    TINA
You need to watch what you say.

                    JIMMY
Hey, who's Mercedes Masterson anyway? Is she a
new girl?

                    SHELLY
                    (Angry)
Where you looking through our mail again?

                    JIMMY
I didn't open anything?

                    TINA
You better not have or I'll bop you one.

(SHELLY finds her letter and is elated)

                    JIMMY
I guess I'll see you all later.

(He exits and rides off on motorcycle)

                    TINA
I don't know what Sam sees in that guy.

                    SHELLY
                    (Touched)
Oh, Tina, listen to this. "Dearest Mercy,"

                    TINA

Skip to the juicy parts.

                    SHELLY
It's all heavenly. "Mercy. There couldn't be a more
perfect name for you. You are my angel of mercy."

                    TINA

Does it get juicy?

                    SHELLY
"But I have a confession to make."

                    TINA

Oh, dear.

                    SHELLY
"My name isn't really Lincoln Jefferson Jones."

                    TINA

Thank goodness.

                    SHELLY
"I'm afraid I lied to you about a lot of things. I'm not
really a straight A student and I'm not president of the
student body. I'm not even a volunteer at the
hospital. I have to be there as a community service for
getting in trouble at school. But I told you all of this
because I wanted you to like me. Someone as
beautiful and wealthy as you could never like anyone
as terrible as me."

                    TINA

It sounds like you two are made for each other.

SHELLY
"I know you probably want nothing to do with me now
that you know the truth about me. But I knew I
couldn't lie to you forever. I've never met anyone like
you before. I don't think I ever will again. I'm sorry this
has to end so soon. Our last night together is
something I'll never forget."
Isn't it wonderful, Tina?

TINA
I'll say.

SHELLY
He liked me enough to tell the truth. That takes a lot
of guts.

TINA
Sounds like a good catch to me.

SHELLY
He is dreamy.

TINA
So does it get juicy after that?

SHELLY
(Smiles)
Wouldn't you like to know?

TINA
It does?

SHELLY
I'm not telling. It's private.

TINA
Oh, come on, Shelly.

SHELLY
There are some things a girl of virtue will not share.

TINA
Oh, please. Give me a break.

SHELLY
Let's go out to the barn where no one can hear.

TINA
Okay.

(The girls laugh and run off R. LIGHTS FADE TO BLACK)

<u>ACT 2</u>

<u>Scene 3</u>

(Lights come up on SHELLY, TINA, PAULA, and JAMIE sitting or standing outside, looking ill. DR the flowers are in bloom)

TINA
Five days of Sam's cooking.

PAULA
I don't feel so good.

SHELLY
Me neither.

JAMIE
What did they put in those omelets?

SHELLY
I don't want to know.

(PAULA is looking very ill)

TINA
Tasted like onions, peppers...and who knows what...

JAMIE
I think it had some egg too.

(PAULA is looking worse and worse)

TINA
Man was it hot. Fresh out of Mexico.

SHELLY
At least I hope everything was fresh.

TINA
I hope they didn't use that moldy squash.

PAULA
(Yells and runs)
I'm gonna puke.

(PAULA exits R)

                            JAMIE
                     (Feeling ill herself)
          I better see if she's okay.

(JAMIE follows R)

                            TINA
          I hope Ma comes home soon. I can't wait to eat good
          food again.

                           SHELLY
          That is if we survive.

                            SAM
                     (Comes out happily)
          Hi, girls. Like breakfast?
                     (SHELLY and TINA glare)
          It was our special Mexican surprise omelet.

                            TINA
          What's the surprise?

                            SAM
                 (Pulls a clove from her pocket)
          Extra garlic.

                            TINA
                 (Ready to throw up. Runs)
          Oh!!

(SAM bites into it. SHELLY covers her mouth and runs too)

                            SAM
          What's wrong with them?

(JAMIE leads PAULA back on stage)

                            JAMIE
          Feeling any better?

                           PAULA
          No.

                            JAMIE
          Maybe you should rest awhile.

PAULA

Maybe.

SAM

What's with her?

JAMIE

Breakfast didn't settle too well with her.

SAM

It's that wimpy stomach of hers. Can't take a little
heat.

JAMIE

Why don't you go inside Paula?

PAULA

I think I'd rather sit out here. It still smells like
breakfast inside.

(She goes and sits on porch)

SAM

She'll be fine.

JAMIE

Sam, I wanted to talk to you about something.

SAM

Yeah?

JAMIE

I know this is really none of my business...

SAM

But...

JAMIE
(Takes SAM aside)
Are you the one who's...

SAM

Who's what?

                    JAMIE
You know...expecting.

                    SAM
You mean having a baby? No way.

                    JAMIE
Really?

                    SAM
Hey, I ain't stupid. I'm careful.

                    JAMIE
So the home pregnancy test wasn't yours?

                    SAM
Nope.
              (JAMIE looks confused)
Sorry to disappoint you.

                    JAMIE
Then who could it belong to?

                    SAM
I figured it wasn't you.
              (Turns to look at PAULA)
And it's definitely not Paula.
              (Thinks)
So my money is on Shelly.

                    JAMIE
What about Tina?

                    SAM
You want to know the truth?

                    JAMIE
Oh, no. Do I really want to hear this?

                    SAM
              (Stage whisper)
It is my personal opinion that Tina is in love with
Shelly.

                    JAMIE
No way. You mean...

                    SAM
Yup. Tina is really a Tim.

                    JAMIE
You're kidding me.

                    SAM
I'm serious. Just watch her some time. She don't act
much like a girl.

                    JAMIE
I suppose not.
                    (Skeptical)
Are you sure?

                    SAM
Fine. Don't believe me. See if I care.

                    JAMIE
It's hard to believe, that's all.

(SAM looks off L. SHELLY and TINA enter)

                    SAM
Here they come, watch.

(JAMIE rolls her eyes)

                    SHELLY
Look there's chef o' death.

(SAM smiles strangely at them)

                    TINA
                    (Annoyed)
What are you staring at?

                    SAM
Nothing.

(SAM'S smile grows weirder)

                    TINA
Quit staring.

                    SAM
Who me?

                    TINA
Yeah, you with the stupid grin.

                    SAM
Oh, sorry.

                    TINA
You watch it, Sam. I ain't in the mood for it today.

                    SAM
Yes, sir. Sorry, sir.

                    TINA
I oughta punch you now and save me the trouble.

                    SHELLY
Come on, Tina. Ignore her. She's only trying to bug
you.

                    SAM
I believe it's your girls' turn to do dishes.

                    TINA
Yeah, we're goin'. We don't need you to be our mom.

(They start to go)

                    SAM
Bye, girls.
        (TINA glares at SAM as they exit inside)
See!

                    JAMIE
I don't know, Sam.

                    SAM
I still don't think Tina's the one.

                    JAMIE
Who knows? Maybe Shelly got her pregnant.

                    SAM
(Smiles)

Hey, that was pretty funny. I didn't know you made jokes.

                        JAMIE
Every once in a while, I'll come out with a good one.

                        SAM
They're rare, but worth it.

                        JAMIE
Thanks.

                        PAULA
I feel sick.

                        SAM
Still?

                        JAMIE
Let's get you inside and in bed.

(JAMIE takes PAULA inside. SARGE comes out looking over a piece of paper. He reads it carefully. SAM watches him. He finds a mistake)

                        SARGE
Gosh darn-it. How'd I miss that?
                  (Corrects paper)

                        SAM
What-cha doin', Sarge?

                        SARGE
I got somethin' special for you girls.

                        SAM
Like what?

                        SARGE
Ring the bell and you'll find out.

                        SAM
Sure.

(Rings dinner bell. SHELLY and TINA come from off R. JAMIE comes from inside)

SHELLY

What's goin' on?

TINA

You guys didn't cook again, did you?

SARGE

No, I got somethin' special for you.

SAM
(Joking)

Is it money?

SARGE

No.
(Looks around)
Where's Paula?

JAMIE

She's comin'. She's still not feelin' too well.
(PAULA comes out. She looks really ill)
Here she is.

SHELLY

What do you have, Sarge?

SARGE

Well, a certain somebody told me that I don't say very
many nice things to you girls, so I wrote something
nice about each of you. I want to share it with you
now.

(All girls look at each other surprised)

SHELLY

You didn't have to do that.

SARGE

Sure I did. Listen.
(Turns to Sam)
Sam: You are a spunky girl, full of fire.
You will do anything you desire.

JAMIE

It's like a poem.

SARGE

You are smart enough to rule Iran,
And pretty enough to do the Can-can.
                    (Girls laugh)
You are funny even on a rainy day.
What else is there that I can say?

(All the girls clap and cheer)

SAM
(Hugs SARGE)

Thank you, Sarge.

SARGE

You bet.

SHELLY

That was really good.

TINA

Who's next?

SARGE

Paula is.

PAULA
(Shyly)

Me?

SARGE

Come on over here so I can see you.
                    (PAULA walks over reluctantly)
Paula, is it true,
That there is no one
Quite like you.
You are a lot of fun,
And you love Jesus too.
No one is as devout as you.

(Everyone cheers except for PAULA)

JAMIE

What's wrong, Paula?

PAULA
(Starts to cry)
None of that's true.

SARGE
Of course it is.

PAULA
It's all lies.

SHELLY
Paula, Sarge worked hard on these. Don't go and spoil it.

PAULA
But it's wrong. I'm not anything like that.

TINA
What are you talking about?

PAULA
I'm a horrible person. And I'm no Christian.

SARGE
Now, Paula. You're as faithful as anyone here.

PAULA
Don't say that.

JAMIE
Paula, calm down.

SARGE
(Confused)
Did I say something wrong?

SHELLY
No, she's just a spoiled brat.

SAM
Leave her alone.

PAULA
No, let her scold me. I deserve to be hated. Especially by you, Sam.

SAM
(Yelling)
What in the hell are you talking about?!
(Pause. Silence)

PAULA

I sinned with Jimmy.

(Long pause. Everyone is shocked)

SAM
(Venomous)
You what?

PAULA

He said you didn't love him anymore and he needed
somebody to love him.

SAM

My Jimmy?

SHELLY

Does this surprise you?

SAM

Shut up.

PAULA

And he told me I was pretty.

SAM

It was that easy, huh?

PAULA

No one ever told me I was pretty before.
(Pointed at the girls)
All I ever hear is how ugly I am.

SAM

I'm gonna kill him. I'm really gonna kill him.

PAULA

It was my fault, Sam.

                         SAM
I rather doubt it.
                              (Runs off L)
He's dead meat.

                         SARGE
Sam, come back here!

 (SARGE runs after her)

                         PAULA
How could I do such a thing?

 (PAULA burst into tears. JAMIE comforts her)

                         JAMIE
You'll be okay.

                         TINA
So are you pregnant?

                         PAULA
Huh?

                         TINA
The home pregnancy test. Did it test positive?

                         PAULA
I don't know what you mean.

                         TINA
Then it wasn't yours?

                         JAMIE
What?

 (Big pause. JAMIE, TINA, and PAULA look at each
 other, then at SHELLY who has moved away from the
 crowd)

                         TINA
Shelly?

                         SHELLY
I didn't really want anyone to know.

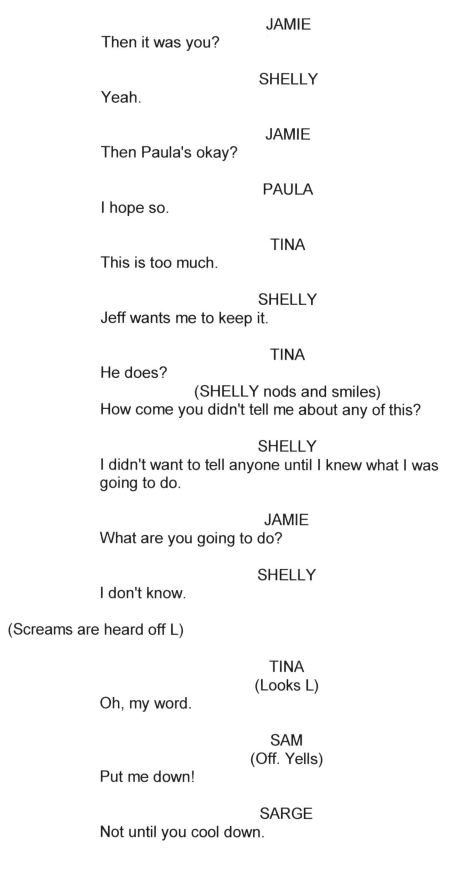

                    JAMIE
Then it was you?

                    SHELLY
Yeah.

                    JAMIE
Then Paula's okay?

                    PAULA
I hope so.

                    TINA
This is too much.

                    SHELLY
Jeff wants me to keep it.

                    TINA
He does?
          (SHELLY nods and smiles)
How come you didn't tell me about any of this?

                    SHELLY
I didn't want to tell anyone until I knew what I was
going to do.

                    JAMIE
What are you going to do?

                    SHELLY
I don't know.

(Screams are heard off L)

                    TINA
                 (Looks L)
Oh, my word.

                    SAM
                 (Off. Yells)
Put me down!

                    SARGE
Not until you cool down.

(SARGE carries SAM on stage either over his shoulder or under his arm)

SAM

I'm gonna kill him!

SARGE

You better calm down, Sam.

SAM

I ain't stoppin' 'til he's dead!

SARGE

Have it your way.

(SARGE carries her off R)

JAMIE

Where's he taking her?

SAM
(Off)

Don't you dare! Sarge!!

TINA

He's gonna drop her in the water trough!

(Splash then scream)

SHELLY

I can't believe he did it. He always said he would, but
he never has.

(SARGE and SAM enter together. SAM is soaked)

SARGE

Feel any better?

SAM
Much.

PAULA
I still don't feel so good.

SARGE
Jamie. Why don't you take Paula up to her room?

                    JAMIE
Sure. Let's go, Paula. I'll make you some more tea.

                    PAULA
And cinnamon toast?

                    JAMIE
I could probably do that.

                    SARGE
That's her favorite. Ma always makes it when she's
sick.
          (JAMIE and PAULA start inside)
And make sure there's plenty of honey in the tea.

                    JAMIE
Okay.

(JAMIE and PAULA close door)

                    SARGE
          (Looks at remaining girls)
Well, this isn't exactly poem atmosphere now.

                    TINA
You can finish after dinner. We gotta go get it started
now.

(TINA goes inside)

                    SHELLY
                  (Quietly)
Thank you, Sarge.
                  (Smiles)
For thinking of us.
                  (Looks at him)
And for listening.
(SHELLY gives SARGE a quick hug and then runs inside)

                    SARGE
I didn't even get to read her poem.

                    SAM
Sarge?

SARGE

Yeah?

SAM

Why do you think Jimmy did that?

SARGE

I don't know, Sam. I didn't think he would. Especially not to Paula.

SAM

They prey on the weak.

SARGE

Nothing I said to that boy must've sunk in.

SAM

It did some good. But not for him.

SARGE

Did he tell you what I said?

SAM

Not really. Sort of I guess. But it still got to me. You could have done a lot worse to him. But you cared enough about me to work something out with him, even though you probably should have clobbered him.

SARGE

I've been talking to his parents and they've been concerned too. We're going to try and find some help for that boy before he gets into big trouble.

SAM

I don't care what you do, just keep him away from me. There's no tellin' what I'll do.

SARGE

Just leave it to me, Sam. We'll get him taken care of.

SAM

Thanks, Sarge.

SARGE

You bet. You better run up and take a shower and
change your clothes before dinner. I'm going over to
talk to Jimmy's parents again.

SAM

Okay.

(SAM goes inside and SARGE exits L. JAMIE and PAULA come out. PAULA
is wrapped in a blanket)

JAMIE

You wanna sit outside?

PAULA

Yeah.

JAMIE

Your tea's almost ready. You sit here and relax. I'll
bring it right out.

(PAULA sits in a chair on the porch. JAMIE exits. JIMMY comes from R)

JIMMY

Hey, Paula. I saw Sarge leaving so I snuck
around. Where's he goin'?

PAULA
(Upset. Pause)
I told him, Jimmy.

(A thousand painful deaths run through his mind)

JIMMY

What?

PAULA

I told him about what we did.

JIMMY
(Wanting it to be a dream)
You did?

PAULA

I told Samantha too.

JIMMY
(He now knows he is dead for sure)
You did?

(JAMIE comes out with tea and toast for PAULA. Sees JIMMY)

JAMIE
You better get out of here, Jimmy. Sam's on the
warpath.

JIMMY
(Remembering to keep his cool)
I ain't worried.
(But he really is)

JAMIE
You should be.

(Front door dramatically flies open. IT'S SAM!)

SAM
Jimmy! You're dead meat!

JIMMY
Wait! I can explain!

(SAM jumps on JIMMY and start punching him. They are on the ground. SAM
hits him. SHELLY and TINA enter to enjoy the fun. Tries to grab her arms)

JIMMY
Stop! Aren't any of you gonna help me?
(Girls watch, enjoying the spectacle)
Help!

SAM
(Punch)
That's for me.
(Punch)
That's for Paula.
(Punch)
And that's just for fun.
(Picks him up and pulls him over
to PAULA)
Now you say you're sorry to her.

(He tries to look hurt, like he is a victim)

JIMMY
I don't know what you mean.

(SAM slaps him in the head)

SAM
Say you're sorry or you'll be sorry.

JIMMY
(Pause)
Sorry, Paula.

SAM
(Pulls him up)
Good, now you die.

TINA
Don't forget the slow torture, Sam.

(JIMMY struggles to get free. SAM is trying to keep control. TINA grabs him too. SHELLY helps also)

JIMMY
Let me go! What's goin' on?

TINA
We are doing a service to women everywhere.

JIMMY
What are you going to do?

TINA
Something painful.

SAM
Something horrible.

TINA
Then we'll kill you.

JIMMY
Help!

                    SAM
Let's go girls! To the barn!

                    TINA
And the tool shed.

                    JIMMY
No!

                    SAM
Coming, Paula?

(An evil look comes over PAULA'S face)

                    PAULA
I wouldn't miss it for a million dollars.

                    SAM
To the barn!

(All the girls except JAMIE march JIMMY off. JAMIE isn't sure what to think.
Smiles. She realizes it could be fun)

                    JAMIE
I've got to see this.

(She runs off R)

                    MA
                (Enters L)
Hello. I'm back.
                (Goes inside)
Hello.
                (Comes out)
Where is everyone?

                    SARGE
                (Enters L)
Hi, honey. Welcome home.

                    MA
It's nice to be home.

(They hug)

SARGE

Have you seen Jimmy? I need to talk to that boy.

MA

No, I haven't seen anyone. What did you do with all the girls?

SARGE

What do you mean?

MA

There's nobody here.

SARGE

Oh, shoot. I was hoping you wouldn't notice.

MA

Notice what?

SARGE

I sold them all to the Gypsies.

MA

How much money did you get?

(They laugh)

SARGE

How did your secret mission go?

MA

Operation Runaway was a success.

SARGE

Operation Runaway?

MA

I'll explain later. Here comes one of the girls.

PAULA
(Off R)

I'll get the duct tape!

(PAULA runs on stage and stops when she sees MA)

PAULA (CONT.)
Ma! You're... uh... home.

MA
Nice of you to notice.

SHELLY
Paula!
(Runs on)
Where's the duct...
(Sees MA)
...tape.

SARGE
What do you girls need duct tape for?

TINA
(Off)
Forget it, Shelly.
(Runs on)
We found a rope.
(Sees MA)
Oh, hi.

MA
What is going on here?

PAULA
Well... uh... we're... uh...

TINA
We're having a rodeo.

SHELLY
Yeah!

TINA
We're doing calf roping.

SARGE
With duct tape?

TINA
That was for the... uh...

                    SHELLY
High jump.

                    MA
High jump.

                    TINA
You know. We were going to do horse jumping.

                    SHELLY
Sure! It's great fun.

                    TINA
We're doing all kinds of things.

                    PAULA
I'm a clown!

                    TINA
We already knew that.

                    JAMIE
                 (Runs on)
What's keeping you guys?
                 (Sees MA)
Oh.

                    MA
Is nobody excited to so me?

                    SHELLY
Of course we are.

(SHELLY hugs MA. Other girls join in a group hug with MA in the
middle)

                    MA
                 (Smothered)
That's enough, girls. Thank you.

                    SHELLY
Is your friend better?

                    MA
Much.

(SAM runs on)

                              SAM
          You've got to see this.
                              (Stops)
          Ooops.

                              MA
          See what?

                              TINA
          We already told Ma about the rodeo.

                              SAM
          Rodeo?
                              (TINA kicks SAM)
          Oh, the rodeo!

                              SHELLY
          Isn't it great to have Ma home, Sam?

(SHELLY hugs MA again and the rest of the girls try to join in but
MA waves them off)

                              SAM
          Yeah. Hi, Ma. Welcome back.

                              MA
          It is nice to be back, I think.
                              (Smiles)
          How was Sarge, girls? Did he behave himself?

                              SAM
          It was hard, but we kept him in line.

                              SHELLY
          He was great, Ma. No problems at all.

(MA points to barn. Sarge looks puzzled. Girls try to look innocent.)

                              MA
          What's that up there hanging from the barn?

                              SARGE
          Looks like a white flag or something.

                    MA
Does anyone know what that is?

                    SAM
Nope.

                    MA
Will you get that down for me, Sam?

                    SAM
But we kinda like it up there.

(Girls start laughing. MA grows annoyed)

                    MA
Samantha. You get that down right now.

                    SAM
Okay, fine. Have it your way.

(SAM exits R. Girls laugh. SAM yells)
                    SAM (OFF)
Do I have to touch it?

(Girls laugh more)

                    MA
What is going on here?

                    SARGE
I have no idea. I wasn't over at Jimmy's that long.

                    MA
You weren't having a rodeo, were you?

                    TINA
Well, no.

                    JAMIE
We did do some roping though.

(They laugh more)

                    MA
Will someone tell me what's going on?

TINA
Here comes our fearless leader. Why don't you ask
her?

MA
(Looks off R)
What is that?
(Sees)
Oh, my.

(SAM comes on carrying the underwear like it belonged to a skunk)

SARGE
That isn't my underwear is it?

SAM
Nope.

(Girls are dying, laughing)

MA
(Almost angry)
Who's are they, Sam?
(SAM can't say she is
laughing too hard)
Either you tell me now or you can tell me out in the
wood shed.

SAM
Okay, okay.

(SAM is trying to control herself. Everyone tries to stop laughing)

MA
Well?

SAM
They're Jimmy's.

MA
What?

SARGE
What did you do to him, Sam?

                    SAM
He's still alive if that's what you mean.

                    MA
What's going on here?

                    SARGE
It's a long story.

                    MA
You know about all this?

                    SARGE
Not completely.

                    MA
What has been going on here?

                    SAM
You wouldn't believe us if we told you.

                    MA
Try me.
                    (Pause)

                    SAM
Who wants to start?

(The girls laugh again. They can't stop. MA sighs)

                    MA
Never mind. It's been a long trip. You girls go inside
and get dinner goin. I'll have Sarge explain.

(Girls exits. Still laughing, almost to the point of crying. For the first time, they
all go together, as a group of friends, united as one)

                    SARGE
Jimmy's been making a lot of trouble.

                    MA
                    (Pointing to underwear)
Those aren't...
                    (Looks away)
No, I don't want to know. Everyone's alive. That's all
that matters.

SARGE

Well, I haven't seen Jimmy anywhere. Now I'm worried.

MA

I'm sure he's fine. I really wanted to talk to you alone...
                    (Hands SARGE a letter)
...because of this.

SARGE

It's from Miyo.
                    (Opens letter. Reads)
Thank goodness they're okay.

MA

Good.

SARGE

They had to move and they finally got their new address.
                    (Looks at MA)
I was pretty worried there.
                    (Reaches for envelope)
She sent another picture.
                    (Gives it to MA)
He even looks a bit like Bill.

MA
                    (Smiles)
Sure does.
                    (Looks at SARGE)
Are you still helping them?

SARGE

I was. I wasn't sure if I should now or not.

MA
                    (Looks back at picture)
Billy would want us to.

SARGE

Yeah, I'm sure he would. He was never one to leave someone hanging.

MA

Thank you for doing all this.

SARGE

It was the least I could do. I'm sure he would have done the same for me here.

MA

I'm sure he would have.

SARGE

You still miss him, don't you?
            (MA nods and sits beside him)
I miss him too.
            (SARGE hugs her. A car is heard off
            L)
Who's that?

MA

Oh, good. I didn't think they were too far behind me. It's a surprise. Jamie!

SARGE

It's your sister.

MA

Jamie's mom.

SARGE

Who's the guy?

MA

Her boyfriend.

(JAMIE comes out. SAM and PAULA tag along)

JAMIE

Yeah?

MA

There's someone here to see you.

(JAMIE looks off L. Her expression becomes angry when she sees who it is)

JAMIE

You told them didn't you?

MA

I had to Jamie. Your mom was worried sick.

JAMIE
(Silent anger)

I thought I could trust you.

MA

Please talk to her, Jamie.
(To SARGE)

Let's go inside.
(To PAULA and SAM)

You too, girls.
(PAULA goes)

SAM

Is that your mom?

JAMIE

Yeah, and her boyfriend too.

MA

Sam.

SAM

I'm coming.

(MA and SAM exit with SARGE, leaving JAMIE to face them alone. CONNIE and TOM enter L)

CONNIE

Hi, honey.

JAMIE
(Cold)

Hi.

CONNIE

How are you?

JAMIE

Fine.

CONNIE

I've been worried about you.

JAMIE
(Not responding)
Uh-huh.

CONNIE
Tom. If you go inside, Betty will introduce you to everyone.

TOM
Okay.

(TOM goes inside)

CONNIE
Jamie? Why did you run away?

JAMIE
You don't seem to want me around anymore.

CONNIE
That's not true. Of course I want you with me.

JAMIE
You haven't acted like it since Tom's been around.

CONNIE
Have you been jealous about the time Tom and I spend together?

JAMIE
It's not that. It seems like you care more about him than you do me.

CONNIE
Jamie, you'll always be my favorite person. No one can ever replace you.

JAMIE
You sure didn't make me feel that way.

CONNIE
Have I been that bad?

JAMIE

It's just that anything I say about Tom is some sort of big crime or something.

CONNIE

I want you to like him.

JAMIE

What for? He'll be gone soon, then they'll be another one.

CONNIE
(Annoyed)
I think we're pretty serious.

JAMIE

You've said that before.

CONNIE

You won't give me a chance will you? I need a life too, you know.

JAMIE

See, that's what I mean. I'm just in the way.

CONNIE

That's not true. I want you with me, but my whole life can't revolve around you.
(Pause)

JAMIE
(Calming down)
So what's so special about Tom anyway?

CONNIE

He's smart. He's funny. We have fun together.

JAMIE

That's it?

CONNIE

And he likes kids.

JAMIE

So?

CONNIE

I have to tell you, not many men want to get involved
with women who have kids. Tom doesn't mind
though. He has one too so he's open to it.

JAMIE

I know your last guy sure didn't like kids.

CONNIE

And I can't love a man who won't like my kid.

JAMIE

Yeah.

CONNIE

So will you come home?

JAMIE

Where is home now anyway?

CONNIE

With Tom. You'll like his house.

JAMIE

I guess. I liked the last guy's house better.

CONNIE

But he wouldn't let you touch anything.

JAMIE

True.

CONNIE

Tom's a great guy. You'll see.

JAMIE

I guess we can give it a try.

CONNIE
(Hugs JAMIE)
Thank you, honey. Let's make it work this time.

JAMIE

We'll try.

CONNIE

Tom will too.

JAMIE

I have to admit something though.

CONNIE

What's that?

JAMIE

I kinda liked it here. It's going to be hard to leave.

CONNIE

Because of Betty?

JAMIE

No, because of the girls.

CONNIE

Really? I heard they were kind of strange.

JAMIE

No stranger than the rest of us.

CONNIE

If you say so.
                    (Looks DR)
Who's garden?

JAMIE

Huh? Oh, Sarge's.
            (Looks. Sees the full grown
            flowers)
Oh, my word...

JAMIE
            (Yells)
Hey, everybody. Come look at this.

(JAMIE rings the dinner bell and SARGE comes out followed by MA, TOM, and PAULA. SHELLY and TINA come from off R)

SARGE

What is it?

JAMIE
Your flowers.

SARGE
(Runs up)
Holy cow. They grew!
(SAM comes out. Smiles)

SHELLY
You're kidding.

TINA
No way.

SARGE
Look!

MA
I don't believe it.

CONNIE
How did you do it?

SARGE
I don't know.

SAM
(Joins them)
He's got a green thumb I guess.

SARGE
No, but I got a crooked one.

(SARGE shows thumb)

TOM
How did you hurt your thumb?

TINA
Oh, no, not the thumb story.

(SHELLY and TINA take off)

                    SARGE
           (SARGE takes TOM for a walk)
It was a baseball accident. I was playing in the minor
leagues...

                    TOM

Really?

(SARGE and TOM exit L)

                     MA

I still can't believe it.

                    SAM

Amazing, isn't it?

                     MA
                (Catching on)
You didn't have anything to do with this, did you Sam?

                    SAM

Who me?

                     MA

Yes, you.

                    SAM

I won't dignify that with a response.

                     MA

What am I going to do with you, Sam?

                    SAM

The question should be, "What would you do without
me?"

                     MA

Life sure would be boring.

                   JAMIE

It sure would.

                     MA

I'll take you up to the guest room, Connie.

                        JAMIE
We staying?

                        CONNIE
For a day or two.

                        JAMIE
Good.

                        MA
I sure didn't think Tom and Sarge would hit it off.

                        CONNIE
I didn't either. You just never know.

(MA and CONNIE go inside)

                        PAULA
Are you leaving, Jamie?

                        JAMIE
Yeah.

                        PAULA
I'm gonna miss you.

                        JAMIE
I'm going to miss all of you too.

                        PAULA
Really?

                        JAMIE
Yes, really.

                        SAM
You'll have to come back and visit.

                        JAMIE
I will. And you can come visit me.

                        SAM
You'll have to come see Shelly's baby.

                        JAMIE
Did she decide to keep it?

                        SAM
They want to. I think they're crazy.

                        JAMIE
Maybe it will be okay.

                        SAM
Stranger things have happened.

                        JAMIE
                        (Smiles)
Yeah, like those flowers there.

                        SAM
                        (Laughs)
Isn't it amazing what a little TLC will do?

                        PAULA
I wonder how he did it?
                (SAM and JAMIE look at
                each other and laugh)
What did I say?

                        SAM
Nothing, Paula.

                        JAMIE
It's a private joke.

                        PAULA
Fine. I have a few private jokes of my own.

                        SAM
You do, huh?

                        PAULA
Yeah, and they're funny too.

                        SAM
I hope so.

                        JAMIE
I wish I didn't have to go.

PAULA

Can't you stay?

JAMIE

No, sorry.

SAM

We'll just have to throw you a going away party. It'll be great. We'll sneak out tonight and borrow the truck...

PAULA

You're gonna get in trouble.

SAM

Not if anybody doesn't tell.

PAULA

What if I do?

SAM

Then you'll wish you hadn't.

PAULA

I will, huh?

(Stage is empty for a few moments. Off R a cry is heard)

JIMMY

Okay, you can untie me now?!
                        (Pause)
Is anybody there? Hello? You guys didn't leave did you? Hello? Anybody? HELLO!

(LIGHTS FADE TO BLACK)

END OF PLAY

MONOLOGUES FROM THIS PLAY

BEAUTY AND PERFECTION

(A light comes up on a small area of the stage R where SHELLY sits alone doing her hair and looking in a hand mirror)

SHELLY

Beauty and perfection. That's what you are Miss Shelly. Bet those boys back home would be doing a quite a bit of howling if they saw you now. Look at all the wonderful things time has done to you.

(Lowers mirror)

And when I get to Hollywood and become a star, they'll wonder where this goddess came from. But my past will be a mystery, because life before this moment ain't worth telling about. After those early years things have only gotten better. Actually I'll bet being born was one of the biggest let-downs of all. I spent all that time wrapped up in that little space in my mama, and for what? I pop out and look around, screaming, wondering if this was such a good idea. Wondering why someone didn't tell me sooner what it was gonna be like those first few years, 'cause if someone had told me, I don't think I woulda come out.

PIGGY PRINCESS

(The light R fades as a light L comes up on PAULA who sits with a baby animal)

PAULA

I've always loved taking care of animals. Horses, cats, dogs, and especially pigs. Momma Nell, one of my foster mothers, used to call me that, her little piggy. And I did look like a little piggy that's for sure. I was plumper than a Buddha doll. Momma Nell used to dress me in pink too. I love how she let me call her Momma. And pink still is my favorite color. One time Momma bought me this most beautiful pink dress for a school. It was all sparkly like pink diamonds. Are there pink diamonds? And the dress had these big old puffy shoulders like Cinderella. I felt like a princess for the whole ride there. I shoulda just turned and gone home cause that was the best part... The boys at the dance said so many mean things to me... they laughed at me... I laughed too... I wanted them to see me laughing... like I wanted to be the joke... I decided piggies shouldn't try to be petunias.

(Smiles, then looks thoughtful and sad)

Momma Nell was the best foster mother I ever had until she got sick. Too sick for me to take care of anymore. I wish they woulda let me try a little longer. I wanted to be there for her like she was for me.

(Puts on a smile)

But I sure know how to take care of animals. That's what I love to do now. I'm like St. Francis of A-sissy.

(Sighs)

And I would sure love to be a saint like Francis, then all this suffering would be worthwhile.

FIRST WORD

(The light fades and comes up R on TINA)

TINA

I watch TV and see those happy families with the little baby who's takin' its first steps or saying its first word. Them folks make such a big deal out of those things. They laugh, they cry... all 'cause they love their little hairless baboon.

(Pause. Grows sad)

And I sit there all that time and wonder... who was there when I took my first step? Who was there when I said my first word?

(Pause)

I doubt if my first word was mama or papa. I'm sure it was four letters though.

(She chuckles a little, then sighs)

I don't care about them... And they don't care about me. But who really cares anyway.

SOB STORY

SAM

Homeless kids aren't homeless because they want to be. Homeless kids are usually ones that aren't wanted. Either their parents died or they left them. Oh, sure there's foster homes but they don't really want you either. If they did, why would they keep getting rid of me? I didn't always have a home. I lived on the streets a little while. And surprise, there were lots of kids there with me. People never thought we were homeless even though we weren't dressed nice. Kids never dress nice anyway. And sometimes we'd even get a five finger discount on something nice from a store. That's how I got caught. I hadn't been out there very long when they got me. Some kids are out there forever. They learn how to survive. I didn't. They gave me a choice. Come here to the Happy Rancher or go to jail. Sarge even came down to visit with me.

(Softens)

He told me about the Happy Rancher and despite the stupid name it sounded kinda cool. And he did something most people never did for me. He asked me what I wanted. He really wanted to know what he could help me do for myself. I just broke down and cried. It seemed like I cried forever. I'd finally found someone who cared.

(Realizes she's just spilled
her guts to a stranger and
makes a total turn around)

Oh, man, what am I saying. You must think I'm a total dork.

(Laughs)

Real sob story, huh?

MESS THINGS UP

SAM

Why do I always do this? Why do I always Mess things up.

(Pause)

I get something good then I ruin it.
(Kicks something handy)
I always have to go and spoil things for people. I just try to have a little fun... but... I don't know when to stop. I keep playing... like a little kid who tells a funny joke over and over. They keep saying it 'cause it was funny once so it should be funny a bunch of times. Then when it's not funny any more, they don't know how to quit. They keep trying, hoping it will still be funny. They keep on joking until someone gets mad and... hurts you.

(Pause)

I'm always playing games. I can't stop.

(She has trouble speaking)
I... can't... stop.

(SAM gains control again)

I always hurt someone. My daddy left because of me.

(Sees reaction)

He did. I found a letter he wrote my mama. He said he didn't want to be tied down by a kid.

(Chokes)

Mama said it was for the best.

(Sad)

But I ran Mama off too. She had better things to do than to sit around playing my games.

SAM (CONT.)

(Looks at house)

And I'm still playing my little games. I should have listened to you. You got a good head. You stopped playing games when you were two or three I bet. Adults always like you... Me? I get 'em to like to hate me. Get 'em so worked up they want nothing but to have me gone.

You gotta admit, I do it well.

(Sits. Trying to control her crying)

I'm sure you've got better things to do than listen to me.

(SAM looks away)

I wanna be alone okay? Please ... Go. Run far away... Like everyone else.

TARZAN

SARGE

Growing up, I did a lot of stupid things too. Maybe not as crazy as Tarzan, but I was wild. See my mother died when I was real young and my pappy didn't want to take care of me. So my family sent me around, hoping somebody could handle me, but I only got worse. My big moment was in a barn too. But I burnt it down. That's when my Aunt Minnie took me in. And for the first time somebody loved me no matter what I did wrong. Even though I didn't change overnight, that love stuck with me. And as I grew older, that love become more and more a part of me until all the hate was gone.

ADAPTED SCENE FOR 2 ACTORS

LINCOLN JEFFERSON JONES

TINA
I'm glad to have you back. I don't think I could have handled these screwballs by myself much longer.

SHELLY
I'm pretty much glad to be back. I'm gonna miss one thing though.

TINA
What's that?

SHELLY
Mr. Lincoln Jefferson Jones.

TINA
Who?

SHELLY
The most gorgeous hunk o' boy my eyes ever feasted on.

TINA
He ain't a doctor is he?

SHELLY
Nope, not yet anyway. Jeffy was a volunteer there.

TINA
Jeffy?

SHELLY
That's what I called him.

TINA
How did you meet him?

SHELLY
Jeffy volunteered at the hospital as a service to the community. He says he's always trying to find ways to help people.

TINA
I know how he could help you.
(They laugh)

SHELLY
He's so perfect. Straight A's and student body
president.

TINA
He ain't a geek?

SHELLY
No, honey, he's fine.

TINA
So what kind of service did he do for you?

SHELLY
We just did a lot of talking.

TINA
Yeah, right.

SHELLY
(Winks)
And maybe a little more.

TINA
I knew it.

SHELLY
But it all was very proper. 'Cause I'm a proper kind of
girl.

TINA
You are?

SHELLY
(Hits TINA)
When I want to be.

TINA
So what did you do?

SHELLY
Be patient. One step at a time.

TINA
Okay. How did it get started?

SHELLY
He was the one that delivered flowers to all the
rooms. I saw him all the time and smiled when he
went by. I guess I did enough smiling, 'cause one day
he stopped with some flowers for me.

TINA
Who from?

SHELLY
Him.

TINA
Score!

SHELLY
"They were left over," he said. He thought I might like
some. That's when the talkin' started. I told him my
name was Mercedes Masterson.

TINA
You didn't.

SHELLY
I did. He called me Mercy for short.

TINA
Heaven help us.
(They laugh)
What else did you tell him?

SHELLY
I said I was a cheerleader and a tennis champ. I said I
go to a private girls' school in California and I let him
know I sure miss boys out there.

TINA
Go, Shelly, go.

SHELLY
(In a high class voice)
That's Mercy, dear.

TINA
Is that how you talked?

SHELLY
Of course, dear.
(Laughs, back to normal voice)
It drove him wild.

TINA
What else did you tell him?

SHELLY
That I was very lost and confused and I needed some
guidance. My mum and my dad were never around
and I really needed someone to help me.

TINA
This is better than TV.

SHELLY
He wanted to help so bad. He was a sweetie.

TINA
Is this where the kissing comes in?

SHELLY
Mercy looks for the finer qualities in men.

TINA
Yeah, right.

SHELLY
He knew I was leaving so he snuck in last night.

TINA
Yeah?

SHELLY
It was nice.

TINA
That's all?

SHELLY
What more do you want? You want me to tell it to you
blow by blow?

TINA
Why not?

SHELLY
Forget it. There are some things we never tell.

TINA
Since when?

SHELLY
Since I met Jeffy.

TINA
Did you get his number?

SHELLY
Yeah.

TINA
Did he ask for yours?

SHELLY
Yeah, but I told him mummy would be furious.
Mummy wants me to marry someone that's really,
really rich. But I said I couldn't stand all those rich
jerks. But if I don't marry one, I lose all of my money.
And you know what he said?

TINA
What?

SHELLY
"Money doesn't matter, only you."

TINA
This is too good to be true.

SHELLY
(Smiles)
I know.

TINA
Are you going to call him?

SHELLY
I don't know if I should.

TINA
Why not?

SHELLY
It was fun at the time, but I don't...

TINA
You got a hot one. Don't lose him now.

SHELLY
We'll see.

TINA
You're crazy to let this one go.

SHELLY
I guess.

(Tina finds something in the flowers)

TINA
Hey, there's a note hidden in here.

SHELLY
Those are the flowers I found this morning when I
woke up. He left them while I was sleeping.

TINA
A love letter! Read it.

(Shelly opens it)

SHELLY
(Touched)
Oh, Tina, listen to this. "Dearest Mercy,"

TINA
Skip to the juicy parts.

SHELLY
It starts out so heavenly. "Mercy. There couldn't be a
more perfect name for you. You are my angel of
mercy."

TINA
Does it get juicy?

SHELLY
"But I have a confession to make."

TINA
Oh, dear.

SHELLY
"My name isn't really Lincoln Jefferson Jones."

TINA
Thank goodness.

SHELLY
"I'm afraid I lied to you about a lot of things. I'm not
really a straight A student and I'm not president of the
student body. I'm not even a volunteer at the hospital.
I have to be there as a community service for getting
in trouble at school. But I told you all of this because I
wanted you to like me. Someone as beautiful and
wealthy as you could never like anyone as terrible as
me."

TINA
It sounds like you two are made for each other.

SHELLY
"I know you probably want nothing to do with me now
that you know the truth about me. But I knew I
couldn't lie to you forever. I've never met anyone like
you before. I don't think I ever will again. I'm sorry this
has to end so soon. Our last night together is
something I'll never forget."
Isn't it wonderful, Tina?

TINA
I'll say.

SHELLY
He liked me enough to tell the truth. That takes a lot
of guts.

TINA
Sounds like a good catch to me.

SHELLY
He is dreamy.

TINA
So does it get juicy after that.

SHELLY
(Smiles)
Wouldn't you like to know?

TINA
It does?

SHELLY
I'm not telling. It's private.

TINA
Oh, come on, Shelly.

SHELLY
There are some things a girl of virtue will not share.

TINA
Oh, please. Give me a break.

SHELLY
Let's go out to the barn where no one can hear.

TINA
Okay.
(The girls laugh and run off R)

END OF SCENE

ADAPTED SCENE FOR TWO ACTORS

WEIRD

JAMIE
Paula? Are you okay?

PAULA
(Sobbing)
Yes, I'm fine.

JAMIE
Did something happen, Paula?

PAULA
Jimmy's naked.

(She covers her face and cries)

JAMIE
He's what?!

PAULA
Naked. He's in the barn swinging around. He thinks
he's Tarzan.

JAMIE
(Trying not to laugh)
Oh.

PAULA
It was awful.

JAMIE
I'll bet it was.

PAULA
(Pause. Grows quieter)
I've never seen a boy naked before.

JAMIE
(Gets a disgusted look on her face)
And Jimmy was the first.

PAULA
What do you think about Jimmy?

JAMIE
Jimmy?

PAULA
Yeah. You think he's okay?

JAMIE
Well, let's just say if he and I were Adam and Eve, I'd
probably do the world a favor and not reproduce.

PAULA
So you don't like him?

JAMIE
Let's just say he's not my type.

PAULA
Oh.
(Looks upset)

JAMIE
Why do you ask?

PAULA
Well, Jimmy was saying all kinds of stuff to me in
there. Stuff I've never thought of before and well... I
kind of liked some of it.

JAMIE
Oh.

PAULA
You know, I've never even been on a date. I mean
being single was fine for Jesus and all, but I got
special needs. Is that bad of me to think that way?

JAMIE
Well, no...

PAULA
I'd really like to get to know a boy. Hold his hand.
(Embarrassed)
Kiss him...

JAMIE
I don't think Jimmy's quite what you have in mind.

PAULA
I guess not, but there really isn't anybody else.

JAMIE
You go to church don't you?

PAULA
Yeah.

JAMIE
Don't you like any guys there?

PAULA
They all think I'm weird. Heck, they think all of us are
weird. The only one of us they'll have anything to do
with is Shelly and we all know why they like her.

JAMIE
Why's that?

PAULA
'Cause she's pretty.

JAMIE
You're pretty.

PAULA
Not like that.

JAMIE
No, but in your own special way.

PAULA
But guys don't want special.

JAMIE
Some do.

PAULA
I haven't met any.

JAMIE
One will come along.

PAULA
You think so?

JAMIE
Sure.
(PAULA smiles)
Tell you what. Why don't we go up to your room and
I'll show you just how pretty you are. We'll put some
make-up on you, do your hair, and find a dress that
compliments your better qualities.

PAULA
I don't know.

JAMIE
Come on. It'll be fun. And if you don't like it, you can
wash it all off.

PAULA
(Smiles)
Jamie?

JAMIE
Yeah?

PAULA
Why are you being so nice to me?

JAMIE
What do you mean?

PAULA
Nobody else here cares. At least not any of the girls.

JAMIE
I'll have to tell you, Paula. Not everybody is like the
girls you live with here. There are some pretty nice
people out there. Sometimes they're hard to find, but
they're there.

PAULA
I'm sure glad I found one of them.

JAMIE
I am too. Let's go.

END OF SCENE

For permission to perform the play, a scene or monologue, contact doug@freedrama.net

Made in the USA
Lexington, KY
19 September 2014